God bless,

The
BLESSING
MAKER

How God Can Turn Your Nothing into Something
and Your Something into Everything

DR. MARK E. STRONG

Foreword by
Dr. Bruce Wilkinson

Interior Design and Typesetting: Katherine Lloyd, the Desk

ISBN-13: 978-1983687723

ISBN-10: 1983687723

Subject: Religion / Christian Life / Family

Printed in the United States of America

First Edition 2018

18 19 20 21 22 23   6 5 4 3 2 1

CONTENTS

FOREWORD

ew things in life are more exhilarating than a God-given
dream. It fills your soul with fresh air. It is like a fragrant,
life-giving breeze that wakes your heart to the possibility that
God can work miracles through your life when you give Him
permission. And that possibility? Well, it can change your life.

I'm sure you've noticed: our world is suffocating. God's
dreamers are needed. The people we love—the people who
God loves—are gasping for His life-giving breath. Though
they may not use those words, their hearts are longing for His
miracles to turn their brokenness into wholeness, their darkness into light, their mourning into dancing.

To turn their hunger into fullness.

My friend, God wants to use you for this. You are the
dreamer your loved ones are waiting for. God's miracles will
flow through you, and this book will help.

In *The Blessing Maker*, Mark will help awaken the dream
and passion God has placed in your heart to serve Him. Step
by step, he will walk you through an incredible miracle of
Jesus—in the Bible and in your own life. Before your eyes,
practical principles and insights born out of Mark's years of
study, his personal life, and ministry will emerge. You will find

yourself yearning and ready for action as the obstacles you face in fulfilling your vision or dream are removed one by one. Most of all, you will be surprised to learn how God wants to use the little you have to meet the need you face.

When Mark was writing this book, he asked me if I would read through the first several chapters. I admit—I was buried in other projects and was a bit tired. However, as I read these pages, my weariness began to give way to a fresh wind of inspiration and encouragement. My prayer for you is that your heart will experience that same inspiring, encouraging breeze. The life-giving breath of God will fill your heart with miracles to bless your life and the lives of others.

May God richly bless you, and let the miracle of *nothing* becoming *everything* in your life begin now.

Bruce Wilkinson

New York Times best-selling author: *The Prayer of Jabez, Secrets of the Vine,* and *A Life God Rewards.*

INTRODUCTION

'll never forget sitting in church on a Sunday morning and listening to Pastor Chester Staples tell the story of God's provision to him and his traveling companions.

It was over one hundred degrees. Pastor Chester and several others stood on the side of the road—waiting. Their broken-down vehicle sat out of commission in the middle of the Mojave Desert. With no place to go to find relief, all they could do was use any available cloth to wipe the dripping perspiration from their faces, and create makeshift fans from anything that could move air. But their ingenuity was no match for the relentless desert heat.

The repair was slow. With each tick of the clock, the breathless desert was gradually suffocating Pastor Chester and the others. Their normal, effortless breathing had been replaced with short, half-desperate puffs and quiet sighs. Their shirt collars and sleeves were drenched with sweat. And hours passed. The arms that once fanned vigorously were now hanging limp only to rise occasionally to give an half-hearted swipe in the air. Frustration and worry had set in. You could see in each of their eyes the growing concern for their welfare.

Chester felt like he was wilting. But he racked his brain trying to figure out how he could be a blessing to his traveling companions. He had a lot of ideas, but the problem was he didn't have enough of anything to make the situation better. He didn't have extra water and sure didn't have a bag of ice laying around anywhere. Nor did he have a high-powered fan or a reflective tent to pop up for some high-tech shelter. However, he knew in his heart, God didn't want him and the others to perish out in the desert. But he had nothing that could help.

Or so he thought.

In desperation, Chester began to whisper, *"O Lord, please help us. O Lord, please help us."* He prayed, but nothing dramatic happened other than a simple song began to swell within his heart. Chester loved to sing, so without even thinking, he began to sing the song loud enough for everyone to hear:

O Lord breathe on us,
let the wind of your Spirit
blow over our souls.

The people standing around him thought he might be losing it. They gave him a collective stare that seemed to ask, "Sir, are you alright?" They figured under these circumstances he would be wise to conserve his energy by foregoing the singing. For the life of them, they couldn't figure out why he would waste his breath, singing a song about wind. Chester ignored their puzzled stares and continued singing anyway,

O Lord breathe on us,
let the wind of your Spirit
blow over our souls.

About the fourth time through his heartfelt song, something unexplainable happened. Out of nowhere, a gust of wind began. A gift from God—a needed blessing! A welcomed cool breeze gently brushed their faces. As the breeze flowed, the group felt immediate relief. Bright smiles stretched across their sun-beaten faces. They knew in that instant that everything was going to be fine.

And everything was.

See, in those heated moments in the desert, something happened in Chester's life that he never imagined. Chester became a blessing maker.

Far As the Curse Is Found

The book you are holding is a very simple window into a very profound truth: God wants to partner with His people to bless them and their world in the midst of deep need.

Chester's example shows the basic truth. In the middle of real need, he simply offered the nothing that he had to God. A simple song! And God turned his *nothing* (his song*)*, into *something* and his something into *everything* that was needed in that moment (a refreshing wind). This is a quiet truth that moves my heart.

This truth exists because of our deep need for God's help in the midst of life's struggle and trials. Penned in the second verse of the Christmas carol "Joy to the World" are the familiar and beloved words:

*He comes to make
his blessings flow
far as the curse is found.*

Here's a fact: because of the effects of sin, we do not live in a world as it should be. The curse of sin runs deep and wide. And every day, every one of us sees or experiences the fallout of living in a fallen world. Tentacles of need seem to reach up from dark waters, wrapping themselves daily around our souls, our bodies, our families, our churches, our communities. The reality is that the old curse is visible. It's usually quite easy to find. But the good news is, like the song says, "he comes to make his blessings flow far as the curse is found." The apostle Paul puts it like this, "Where sin abounded, grace did much more abound (Rom. 5:20b, KJV). Yes, wonderful abounding grace for our salvation and redemption. But also, grace and blessing to meet all our human needs too!

Now the question is, how does God deliver His blessings to heal the empty, painfully jagged wounds caused by the curse? How does He channel the river of blessing into our caverns of need?

You may be tempted here to answer by simply saying, God can make His blessings flow any way He wants. After all, He is Almighty God, and He doesn't need assistance from any human being to do anything! While that is definitely true, there's a bit more to it. The Scriptures clearly teach us that, although God is omnipotent, His delivery system to disperse blessing is not purely His solo act. He chooses *not* to work alone. But what's even more astonishing is who He chooses to work with to deliver His blessings. He chooses partners who are not experts or totally proficient, but He collaborates with those who understand that in order for God to do His work He needs them.

Ephesians 2:10 tells us, *"For we are God's handiwork, created in Christ Jesus to do good works, which God prepared in advance for us to do"* (NIV).

So the correct answer to the question: Through you and me! Sure, God is the Ultimate Blessing Maker and the Giver of all blessings—let's be explicitly clear about that. However, He needs your help to deliver the blessing packages. And let's make no mistake about that either.

Friend, Jesus wants you to be a blessing maker. Through your place of challenge or need, Jesus is extending a life-changing invitation for you to join with Him in sharing His abundant grace in creative ways with the world around you. He's inviting you to give Him what you consider nothing, and to join with Him in His work of blessing those who deeply need God's work or intervention on their behalf.

Let me be honest here. This idea could be used to gloss over life's pain with a false hope, manipulating God into giving what we demand. This is not what it means to be a blessing maker. My purpose in this book is *not* to schmooze you with some slick how-to to teach you to coerce God into giving what you want. You're too smart for that, and I know better. *The goal is synchronization, not manipulation.* It's coming into alignment with God's abundant and generous heart, not getting stuff from a divine vending machine. The blessings God will lavishly pour out are about serving and meeting needs, surely, but they always point hearts toward Jesus and each other, in the mission that reflects His love for all people and creation.

Far from being the end of the story, what you or I consider

"nothing" can be the very thing God uses to perform extraordinary miracles within our lives and beyond. It gives Him the space to show us a God-sized dream and release God-sized miracles and blessings. This is the truth, and we'll spend the rest of the book talking about it.

To highlight that truth, I want to share with you ten life-tested "movements" that God uses to make His and your dream to bless others come true. These movements are not recipes or spells: they are acts of obedience. When we respond to God's commands and leading, He works. Like simple steps of a child toward a parent, these movements are small, doable actions we take to become blessing makers and participate in fulfilling God's dream in our lives and communities, especially if our resources are insufficient.

Do you desire to experience God's amazing work in your life? Do you want to be a blessing maker who works in harmony with God to bless your life and the lives of others? Then walk with me for a little while. We'll go a little closer to our loving Father, who gives good gifts to his children (James 1:17). Our first movement will take us to a sun-swept beach in Galilee to take a close look at a miracle of provision modeled by that Father's perfect Son. We'll watch as Jesus blesses the multitude by turning nothing into something, and something into what seemed like everything.

You may think you know this famous story—The Feeding of the Five Thousand. But I think there is still a surprise waiting for you there. A surprise that, step by step, will lead you to a revelation of God's work, dream, and provision for His blessing makers in this world.

And if you're like me, you'll never look at what you don't have the same way again.

Chapter 1

FROM YOUR DREAM TO GOD'S DREAM

The number of those who ate was about five
thousand men, besides women and children.

MATTHEW 14:21 (NIV)

A blessing maker is first and foremost a dreamer. However, not just any kind of dreamer, but a dreamer who dreams a special, specific dream—God's. Blessing makers are people who have let God blow their mind, and they want more. Let me explain.

I'm a child of the 1970s. If you gave me a dime for every '70s song I can sing by heart, I'd be a very rich man. One of my favorite songs was recorded by The Delfonics, part of the big Philadelphia Soul sound. Every time that song came on the radio, I would tune up my falsetto to dizzying heights and squeak out the chorus:

Didn't I blow your mind this time, didn't I?
Didn't I blow your mind this time, didn't I?

I thought I sounded pretty good—though, for the life of me I couldn't figure out why friends and family would leave the room during my melodic serenade.

To blow someone's mind is the definition of surprise. It means you do something for a person he or she could never expect, not in a million years. "Mind-blowing" is the right description for God's dream for us and this world. His dream, from our vantage point, is unimaginable!

Generally, when we talk about dreams, the conversation centers around *our* dreams. We have our personal dreams, of course—good dreams—for our future, our kids, our ministries, our businesses. The list goes on. There is absolutely nothing wrong with our dreaming. It is good that we dream. God wired us to do just that—pursuing His mission and plan in the turnings of our lives.

We're used to considering ourselves as dreamers. But did you know God is too?

Our God's dream for the world is restoration in Jesus (2 Cor. 5:18–20). But that Great Dream breaks down into many smaller dreams necessary to make it happen, and that's where you and I come in. With that big goal in mind, God's Master Dream sets millions—billions—of smaller dreams into motion. Your dream. Mine, too.

But when was the last time you thought about finding and fulfilling God's dream? When did you last focus your passion, your energy, on seeking what He dreams about? The truth is that *we're prone to forget that we dream because God dreams. And for the record, God is no ordinary dreamer.* He is the incredible, awesome God of all the universe. He is the creator of the majestic splendors in the earth and the sky. He is limit-less and boundless and nothing is impossible for Him—God our redeemer, the Master Dreamer! And best of all, the Master Dreamer wants to include you in His mind-blowing dream. It is a big dream—a dream He yearns for you to embrace and live out. One that impacts your life, that is specific and good and tailor-made for the needs of the weary world. A dream that will cause you to be a blessing maker to those around you by:

- Blessing and meeting the needs of people.
- Demonstrating His love and grace to those who need it.
- Deepening human relationships with Him.
- Causing miracles to happen to strengthen faith and provide.
- Making Jesus visible to a dark world.

Think about a time when you surprised a loved one or a dear friend with a heartfelt gift. Do you remember what made that gift extra special? Likely, it was not just the object or experience, but the careful *thought* it took to pull the surprise off. It took time. You had to figure out exactly what to buy, make, or do for them. Then, you worked to present your gift with the kind of creativity and meaning that such a special thing deserved. And yes, the hardest task of all was probably keeping the surprise a *surprise*! Especially if the recipient was a bit nosey, or should I say, "hyper-inquisitive." But part of the gift was that element of surprise.

Sure, I'm stating the obvious, but what makes a good surprise special is that the recipient doesn't know what has been prepared for them. They are caught off guard by love, ambushed by thoughtfulness. When they receive your gift, their mind is blown. You see their face, and start humming in your best falsetto,

Didn't I blow your mind this time, didn't I?
Didn't I blow your mind this time, didn't I?

Friend, God has been preparing such a surprise for you. God's surprise gift for you is to join Him as He pours out His blessings. He is personally inviting you to be a blessing maker, because He is *the* Blessing Maker He wants you to be a dreamer, because He is the Master Dreamer. He wants you to help Him fulfill His mission in the world by living out your part in it.

This is amazing. But does it always happen? No. It is an invitation that is present for each of us, but just because an invitation exists doesn't mean that we will say yes to it.

Embracing God's dream requires us to understand His heart and say yes to the characteristics that shape His dream. We need to understand that He works differently than the world, and He sees things differently than we do.

It would be impossible for us to try to read the mind of God, but fortunately for us, we don't have to figure it out by ourselves. In the story of The Feeding the Five Thousand, Jesus and His disciples (oh, and a little boy with a simple bagged lunch) reveal incredible insights into God's dream that allow us to embrace it with our whole soul. Let's take a quick peek at the passage and then unwrap the unique pieces of God's dream. If you're familiar with this story, try to clear your mind and hear it for the first time.

> When Jesus heard what had happened, he withdrew by boat privately to a solitary place. Hearing of this, the crowds followed him on foot from the towns. When Jesus landed and saw a large crowd, he had compassion on them and healed their sick.
>
> As evening approached, the disciples came to him and said, "This is a remote place, and it's already getting late. Send the crowds away, so they can go to the villages and buy themselves some food."
>
> Jesus replied, "They do not need to go away. You give them something to eat."
>
> "We have here only five loaves of bread and two fish," they answered.
>
> "Bring them here to me," he said. And he directed the people to sit down on the grass. Taking the five loaves and the two fish and looking up to heaven, he gave thanks and broke the loaves. Then he gave them to the disciples, and the disciples gave them to the people. They all ate and were satisfied, and the disciples picked up twelve basketfuls of broken pieces that were left over. The number of those who ate was about five thousand men, besides women and children. (Matt. 14:13–21, NIV)

Incredible story, isn't it?

What a miracle. Although the story is traditionally called "The Feeding of the Five Thousand," that title is misleading. Jesus and His crew had the daunting task of feeding a great deal more than five thousand people. Way more.

The Bible says there were five thousand *men* present. Not included in the count were women and children. While we can't say for sure exactly how many woman and children were present, we can make a good estimate. Conservatively, we could guess there were probably as many women present as men—give or take a few. And since it was a family affair, the kiddies were out in full force—maybe two, three, or four to a family. So, if we do the math, it was not The Feeding of the Five Thousand, but possibly (likely, even) the feeding of the fifteen-to-twenty-thousand. For perspective, that is close to the average number of people who attend a NBA game. A lot of hungry people. A need worthy of a God-sized dream and a God-sized blessing.

God's Dream Is Mind-Blowing

Wow, what a miracle. Yes, God blew their minds that time. Maybe yours, too, as you read the passage. If so, in a round-about way you have just articulated the first piece of God's dream. God's dream, you see, is mind-blowing, in the way only true miracles can be.

Miracles are acts or signs from God that go against the typical order of things—the common way that natural processes or events progress. And boy, was this one or what? Think about it. There was no way the disciples could stretch those two fish and five loaves of bread to feed teeming masses of people. The math could never work. The limited molecules that made up the flesh of the fish and the baked dough of the bread could never be enough—not enough in a million years. Their perspective of the situation was far different than Jesus.'

For them, the hunger situation was not a divine blessing or dream but a headache and an impossibility. Maybe even a nightmare to some of the disciples torn between the impossible task and a desire to help a hungry throng. But God had a dream.

That dream went beyond reason or rationality. It seemed impossible—until it happened. It didn't make sense by any human logic. It superseded their collective cognitive, emotional, and imaginary faculties. His dream was for the multitudes to experience His love and mercy in provision for their hunger and great need.

That's the way our God works. His dream never fully fits within our capabilities to understand. Our temptation is to shrink-wrap difficult issues and needs, oversimplifying them because they overwhelm our capacities to respond or understand. That's what the disciples were doing when they told Jesus they didn't have enough money to purchase food for the multitude and made the urgent request for Him to send them away. Like us at times, they had developed an acute case of amnesia. They forgot God was bigger than them.

God's dream through Jesus was not held back by the disciples' limitations or lack of miraculous imagination. They were simply victims of short-term amneisa. It escaped their memory, even while traveling with Jesus, that God dreams big dreams, and gives them to small people, to express His big love for all humanity. They had seen, time and again, His power to transform a situation. But they acted like they'd forgotten it.

Don't we forget, too?

In Ephesians 3:20 and 1 Corinthians 2:9–10, the apostle

Paul stamped an exclamation point on the truth about our big God with these powerful words:

Now to him who is able to do immeasurably more than all we ask or imagine, according to his power that is at work within us. (Eph. 3:20, NIV)

However, as it is written: "What no eye has seen, what no ear has heard, and what no human mind has conceived"— the things God has prepared for those who love him— these are the things God has revealed to us by his Spirit. (1 Cor. 2:9–10, NIV)

Both these verses beautifully illustrate my point: God's dream, in keeping with His greatness, challenges our ability to understand it. What He envisions for our situation and future is far beyond our comprehension or imagination—mind-blowing!

If I could put an urban spin on this extraordinary piece of God's dream for my church in Northeast Portland, Oregon, Paul's words would translate (roughly) like this:

God is a dreamer.
The enormity of His dream includes you,
and it will knock you off your feet.
It's so incredible that what He's dreaming
has never, ever crossed your mind.
His dream is so out of this world
you would never even know how to ask for it!
But the cool thing is,
He will reveal His dream to you,

and He will work in you to make it all happen.
Know for sure,
God's dream will blow your mind.
Hallelujah!

God's Dream Is Intimate and Personal

While God's dream to work around and through His people
is mind-blowing and big, it is also intimate and personal. His
dream is big enough to include all of us, yet personal enough
to intimately pay attention to *each* of us. He meets the intri-
cate, individual needs of those He loves.

A friend of mine is the lead pastor of a church in Cali-
fornia. Once, he told me the story of how God first captured
his heart. He'd grown up in a Christian household with two
godly parents, but by the time he reached his teenage years he
decided the Jesus way of life was not for him.

It's a story that has played out a million times. You've
probably heard it—or lived it—yourself. The decision to walk
away from Jesus began a domino effect of inward rebellion.
As my friend turned his back on Jesus, all "God stuff" molted
like geese and flew south for the winter. His body went to
church, but his heart and soul never entered the building. His
attitude toward God and others soured. He became cynical
and jaded. He'd become so proud that he practically sweated
arrogance.

Then the story changed. One day on a hunting trip with a
relative, he was "chilling out" underneath a tree. He lay there
in the middle of nowhere, his mind wandering. Certainly he
was not thinking about God. But God was thinking about

him. As my friend lay beneath the waving branches, watching light filter through the leaves, he had an experience that seemed to come from outside him.

In his mind, he saw the top of heaven. Then, in a flash of glory, he saw a blazing light fall, traveling swiftly from the pinnacle of heaven through the universe, searing past the stars and through the blackness, cutting through the clouds and the sky, descending, descending, reaching, reaching, until it touched him, sitting precisely where he was, underneath the tree. That vision, how far the light came to reach him, devastated his pride and broke his rebellion. It was what he needed to see.

In those few seconds, God showed him the foolishness of his pride, the ridiculousness of his arrogance. He saw clearly just what a microscopic blip he was in the universe. But the light had touched *him*. Radiating from that brief vision was a powerful of message of love. In his heart, it was as if God was saying, *"Son, though you are so small, I love you. I know you. I have a dream I want to share with you."* That unspoken voice rocked him to his core. It was revealed to his heart that the all-powerful God was concerned about him. That He intimately knew him. It set his heart free to embrace God's dream for his life.

What a picture for us. The light from the top of heaven has come down, to each of us. Intimately. Personally. Individually. See friend, God values you. He values me. He values each person so much that He intimately knows the details of their lives. Remember the words of Jesus in Matthew 10:29–30?

Are not two sparrows sold for a penny? And not one of

them will fall to the ground outside your Father's care.
And even the very hairs of your head are all numbered.
(Matt. 10:29–30, NIV)

Think about that. Who in your life do you know that well? Who do you love that much? We simply can't comprehend the extent of God's knowledge and love. It is beyond us. I love my wife, Marla, like crazy. I know her so well. However, for the many years we have been married, I have never once known the exact hair count on her head! But God does. Every morning she wakes up and lives with that kind of care, that kind of love from Him. God knows her perfectly, completely, because she means that much to Him. And so do you. So do I. So do all of us living in God's dream.

How does all this relate to provision and the feeding of the five thousand? Deeply. God's miraculous love does not just provide in an abstract or impersonal manner. The One who knows us all gives each of us what we need, with the kind of love that numbers every hair and cares for every sparrow.

On that day on the beach in Galilee, God fed the multitude with the paltry loaves and fish set before Jesus. But His dream wasn't just to fill bellies. He was after much more than that! Included in the miracle was a special kiss of grace that touched the heart of every individual present. Through provision, people knew that they were seen, cared for, and loved. Through Jesus, each dear heart knew that they were loved, valued, and intimately known by God.

For every person who felt that love, God's dream came true.

The Discovery Place of God's Dream

Let me state the amazing obvious: God allows His dream to be discovered before we can fulfill it. God allows us to unwrap the surprise of His dream in the place of our insufficiency. We begin to receive His grace in the very place where our need exceeds our resources. In the case of the disciples, God's dream was wrapped in unattractive paper: five loaves of bread and two fish. The packaging of the miracle was a lunch that was enough for one boy. It wouldn't have filled up a family, let alone a multitude. Entire villages of food wouldn't have fed that crowd. In fact, it wasn't until Jesus began to multiply the miniscule resources that the disciples began to realize that God had a much bigger dream than theirs.

God reveals His dream to us when we are in hard places. But we'd rather He didn't work that way, wouldn't we?

Do you remember the story of Jacob's dream? It's a brilliant example of God's dream coming to meet a need in a hard place. We read the story in Genesis 28:10–15. Jacob had stolen his brother Esau's birthright and was on the run, with Esau threatening to kill him. For refuge, Jacob headed to his uncle's house in the just-far-enough-away land of Haran. On his way, he spent the night in a place called Luz. Worn out and without the comforts of home, Jacob placed a rock under his head for a pillow and slept. Lying there on that hard, lumpy stone, he dreamed. And in his dream, Jacob began to see God's intimate, personal dream for him.

As he dreamed, Jacob saw a stairway resting on earth and reaching all the way to heaven. On that magnificent stairway, Jacob saw the angels of God with angels ascending and descending. Going up. Going down. While viewing this celestial vision, God spoke to Jacob about Himself, His dream for His people, and His personal promise to Jacob. He provided the vision that was needed in a place of total failure and insufficiency.

When Jacob woke, he made a startling statement:

"Surely the LORD is in this place, and I was not aware of it." He was afraid and said, "How awesome is this place! This is none other than the house of God; this is the gate of heaven." (Gen. 28:16–17, NIV)

Wait a minute. Slow it down for a second and rewind! Did you hear what Jacob said about his hard place? He said,

Surely the LORD is in this place...How awesome is this place! This is none other than the house of God.

Wow! The words Jacob spoke tell us unequivocally that something fantastic had happened to him. He saw himself in a new way, saw his circumstances in a new way. God's dream was revealed to him in that hard place. God *chose* a place of insufficiency to show His dream—insufficiency to the point that Jacob didn't even have a pillow to comfort his head while he slept.

About now you may be asking, "Why does God choose places of insufficiency and not enough to reveal His dream to us? Why couldn't He find some softer or happier place to surprise us with His dream?" Friend, there is a beautiful answer to that question, even if it is a hard one.

No one in life ever has everything they need all the time. Even if a person has billions of dollars, they still have needs. Having an abundance of money, or any other thing of value, doesn't make any of us totally self-sufficient. The only all-sufficient one in the universe is God! The rest of us have a big "NS" attached to us, meaning we are NOT SUFFICIENT at some time or another in our life. Every single one of us has needs. And having need is not necessarily bad, because it points us to the One who cares for and loves us the most. So we should remind ourselves that our deep lack pales in the face of God's abundance.

So God in His wisdom chose a road we all travel—our needs and insufficiencies—to place an awesome surprise. He chose a location where everybody could access His dream. He chose the place of "not enough," the unwanted and laughable wrappings of five loaves and two fish, to reveal His dream of abundance, provision, and sufficiency.

That is hard. But it is a gift. A surprise, thoughtfully prepared and packaged. It means you and I will have the opportunity to discover His dream, and so will everybody else. It means that God's dreams and our dreams can align.

It also means that we have to trust Him.

One More Dream Piece

There's one more very important piece of this puzzle: God's dream involves *you*.

You may not have thought of this before, but it is the truth: While you need God to fulfill your dream, God needs you to fulfill His! For some reason, we get this weird, unbiblical notion that God will do His work by Himself. Not true. The Bible teaches clearly that God partners with His people to fulfill His purposes.

God will not fulfill His dream all by Himself. Rather, He *always* works with someone to bring His dream to fruition. God, from the very beginning worked in harmony—the Father, Son, and Spirit being the creative community, working seamlessly together to create all things.

He invites us to join Him in what He is doing in that same spirit of sharing work and community. Just look at the Father's partnership on the beach of hungry people: God uses Jesus (God, yes, but in human form), who uses a little boy who brought a lunch along. Once the disciples embraced the dream, Jesus used them, too, to organize the crowd and distribute the miraculous provision given from the hands of Jesus.

What if God is waiting, *right* now, to use you that way?

God gives us His dream, He then equips us for the dream, and finally He empowers us to live and do the dream. The key to embracing God's dream is understanding that you will need to participate in it. Your active participation is integral. Vital. Necessary.

Struggling with that? Maybe the apostle Paul's words will help:

For there is no difference between Jew and Gentile—the same Lord is Lord of all and richly blesses all who call on him, for, "Everyone who calls on the name of the Lord will be saved."

How, then, can they call on the one they have not believed in? And how can they believe in the one of whom they have not heard? And how can they hear without someone preaching to them? And how can anyone preach unless they are sent? As it is written, "How beautiful are the feet of those who bring good news!" (Rom. 10:12–15, NIV)

Make no mistake about it—Jesus is the gospel, the good news! However, Scripture tells us, if no one preaches the gospel to the lost, they will not hear the message. If the partners of God fail to show up, could it be that the dream of God fails to go out? Could it be that collaboration is essential—even when the need is as basic as the gospel? Could it be, in other words, that for the gospel of Jesus Christ to transform humanity, we must take an active role in sharing it?

Could it really be that the stakes are that high? That so much depends upon our maturity, courage, and obedience? If you, I, and others who are sent fail to preach, what happens to God's dream to reach the lost? Could it be that there is a way in which God has chosen to need us to complete His work?

Hear me now. When I ask if God needs you and me, it gives us no reason for pride or boasting. Instead, as anyone who has partnered with God can tell you, it is a humbling reality. It is an incredible privilege we have been given. This tremendous gift should cause our hearts to be continually bowed in a posture of gratitude and adoration for the simple fact God Almighty sees fit to allow you and me to partner with Him in fulfilling His great dream. Ephesians 2:8–10 sums it up well:

> For it is by grace you have been saved, through faith—
> and this not from yourselves, it is the gift of God—not by
> works, so that no one can boast. For we are God's hand-
> iwork, created in Christ Jesus to do good works, which
> God prepared in advance for us to do. (NIV)

But here is the miracle: God's dream to use us means that our feet are made beautiful as we partner with Him. His dream uses us to bring what we are totally insufficient for: to meet the world's need. And we are made more beautiful in the process, for we are made more like Him.

Many years ago, I was at a pastor's conference. One of the speakers articulated God's need for us to help fulfill His dream by simply stating, "God is a dreamer, but He must find a person who will dream with Him." I can't think of a better way to say this. It is 100 percent right.

I have spent this chapter trying to convince you of a few key truths about God's dream and provision. But in some ways, I feel that I have been sketching them in black and white. Why? Because you will need to provide the color, the detail. You will need to discern with the Holy Spirit what this will look like in your life.

Only you can finish painting the picture of what God's dream for you looks like personally. It will be intimate, exactly what is needed. It will be powerful, aligning with God's heart for the world. But what will that look like? Only you, discerning through God's Spirit, can know. God's dream will only become clear to you as you decide to allow Him to make it happen through you.

The color is yours to discover. Your dream, God's dream, is waiting. Are you ready to partner with Him?

HEART AFFIRMATION

If you're ready to become a blessing maker by receiving God's dream, invite Him to work through you by praying this prayer:

> *God, you are the Master Dreamer. Your dream for me and others is good. I acknowledge that, although you are the Almighty, you need me, you choose me to fulfill your dream. Today I accept that responsibility, and I say yes to the privilege of allowing your dream to become my dream. You and I will work together, and miracles will happen. Thank you for giving me the opportunity to be a blessing maker, though what I have seems to be nothing. In Jesus's name, Amen.*

PART ONE

MOVEMENTS WITHIN

Chapter 2

Movement One:
FROM BLINDNESS
TO REVISION

*And when Jesus went out He saw a great
multitude; and He was moved with compassion
for them, and healed their sick.*
Matthew 14:14 (NKJV)

Just because you have a desire to be a blessing maker doesn't mean it will be easy. Nor does being called or having a dream mean you are going to see everything clearly initially either. In fact, there is a good possibility you may be blind to the very thing God wants you to see—I definitely was.

During my first years as a pastor, I experienced a lot of discouragement. Contributing to my angst was a rather basic problem: I didn't want to be a pastor in the first place. My goal in life had been to be an evangelist and nothing else. I wanted to preach the gospel all over the world, to see thousands come to Jesus. In my mind, being a pastor long-term wasn't the plan, and I was eager to jump ship from my pastoral position as soon as I finished seminary. But God's dream was different from mine. His dream was for me was to be an evangelist, but also to invest my life in a community of people by being a pastor. After a few years of tug-of-war with the Lord, He gave me peace and a deep love for the community I was called to serve. I came to terms that pastoring for me was not a pit stop. It was a destination. It was a calling. And after a few decades, I'm still a happy pastor. However, I still struggled in a number of areas. Like, for example, trying to find a suitable building for our church after circumstances forced us out of our old building.

It wasn't that we couldn't find a building. There were definitely buildings around us that would have worked for us. Plenty of them. Large buildings. Beautiful buildings. Expensive buildings...

Yes, *all* expensive, from my perspective at least. Our problem was resources. We simply didn't have the money to purchase a building or even property. We had nothing. I tried everything I could think of to figure it out, but all my good efforts failed. Our capital campaigns were heavy on the campaign and light on the capital. The dream of having our own space in our neighborhood for worship and ministry seemed impossible.

It was frustrating. I knew that we needed thousands of dollars to acquire a building. But after several months we had only raised hundreds. We tried getting a loan, but we were turned down so many times I nearly developed a rejection complex. The church was stuck. And me? I wasn't a happy camper.

And seven years went by. During that time, our church

met in tents, school buildings, other church chapels and sanctuaries. Our motto was, "if you can find us, you can worship with us!" In that rough season, I became chronically discouraged. Especially since my eye had been on a piece of property that entire time. "Craigo's" was the neighborhood grocery store. At the time, it was the largest store in the neighborhood. It sat on a little over an acre of land in our North Portland neighborhood, historic homes and streets in the blocks surrounding it. The building was about 21,000 square feet. From our community's perspective, it was huge.

During those seven years, I drove by the store all the time. *That place would be great for our church,* I'd daydream. *It's visible. We could serve the community. Everyone knows where it is.*

But why even dream? There was no way we could buy it.

Finally, I just decided to ask and worked up enough nerve to talk to the owner. I wanted to ask if he'd be willing to sell. I must have been crazy. We didn't have enough money in our church account to purchase a used car, let alone Craigo's. But I went and asked him anyway.

"Young man," he said, "you're being a bit ambitious, and the building is not for sale at the moment." I'm still not sure if he was trying to be funny, but after his initial response, he tossed out a price that hit me like a dropped bowling ball. He said, "If you want to buy it, it will cost you $450,000!" That is a large number today, but back then? Forget about it. Wobbling, I told him, "OK, I'll get back to you."

I went to our denominational board. I told them about the building and how it seemed perfect for us. Surprisingly, they encouraged our church to apply for a loan. I couldn't believe it. The owner had jokingly thrown out a price, and there was a possibility that we could get the money.

I met with a loan officer, who said a sentence I never expected to hear. "Mark, we look forward to giving you the loan." The very next day, though, the denominational board met. After consideration, they felt that the building was too large—we were dreaming a bit above our congregational pay grade. They voted against the purchase, saying that we should look for something smaller, less ambitious. I was heartbroken for months. We still had nothing, and my hopes had been raised so high. My frustration and discouragement lingered, until by God's grace, my vision began to change.

Time passed. One day, I had just finished speaking at a men's conference in St. Louis. After my session, many of the men were at the altar pouring their hearts out to the Lord. The Holy Spirit was moving beautifully, and I wanted to spend some time seeking the Lord too. I made my way down the steps and squeezed into an open space in the front of the church.

I began praying. Then weeping. The tears were coming out before I even knew what was happening. My emotion didn't make sense to me. I wasn't sad, but I couldn't stop crying. So I stayed kneeling, and allowed my tears to flow in the presence of Jesus.

After a couple of minutes, a brother named Raphael Green walked behind me. He placed his hand on my shoulder. Then he began to speak: "The tears you are crying are for a people who you have never seen or known. They are for a people that God is going to raise up in your city and community." They were words from God for me. In that brief message, though I was unaware of the impact it would have, a re-visioning began to happen, one that would change my church, community, and life. Deep in my heart a passion ignited on a profound level to reach and serve the people in my city and community. I wanted to love those who Jesus deeply loves. Something clicked—like a dream aligning somewhere. My vision for my church shifted as I knelt from a building focus to a *people* focus. I left St. Louis seeing my ministry much differently— although not knowing or really understanding what had taken place within me.

But when I arrived back in Portland, nothing had changed. Our church still lacked an adequate facility. We still lacked money. The disappointments of the previous years lingered in my soul. We still had "nothing."

But one thing was different. I had begun to see our situation with new vision. Before, I had been fixated on Craigo's. It seemed all-important. But I began to see with more importance the *people* around the store. Most of them were in deep need. As my vision shifted, new sights popped into clear focus: I could really *see* all the crack dealers and addicts who surrounded the building all hours of every day, seven days a week. I could really see the single mothers coming into the store, trying to support their family with meager food stamps. I could really see the johns driving in from the suburbs, picking up girls, then dropping them back off minutes later. And more: I saw youths in the neighborhood in need of Jesus Christ. I saw men who'd lost hope and purpose for life, in real danger of losing themselves to substances or violence.

I could see, for the first time, the store, not as a stepping stone to my ministry dream, but as a cancerous hub in our community that needed to be healed. *This place is a wound that God dreams of healing*, I thought. I saw a community in painful need of the gospel of Jesus Christ. My heart had shifted. Frustration was gone, replaced by a sense of deep brokenness for these hurting people.

"Mark," you may be shouting at this book, "why didn't you see your community like this before? After all, you are a pastor, right?" I did! But my focus on not having the adequate resources, provision, or building to meet the need of the community had eclipsed the people I was called to serve. My sight was fixed on the wrong thing. Thus, my misplaced vision prevented me from seeing what I really needed to see—the people in my community through the eyes of Jesus. I saw that I hadn't even been aware of my real need. I thought my need was for money, for a building, but it was so much more. My core need was to re-vision. To see things God's way.

Where is my attention? This is the first inner question of a blessing maker aligning themselves with God's dream. We all need to go through this process of re-visioning. Our sight needs to be conformed to Jesus's sight, our dream to God's dream. Blessing makers see through God's eyes and not their own. It is not enough for us to want good things, we need to want *God's* things. And how can we tell the difference if we aren't even seeing the world like He does?

I call this process a "movement." Why? Because this process takes you to a new place, to a new orientation and relationship with God and the world. Re-visioning moves us, and in so doing it changes our perspective, just like you can look at the same scene from the ground floor and the tenth story and see something totally different. It shifts us from the wrong focal point to the right focal point. It centers our view on the person/s of God's affection—the people He wants to touch—and spotlights where He wants to work. What you see with your eyes affects what you feel in your heart, and what you feel in your heart impacts what you touch with your hands. Re-visioning is the starting place for miracles.

Vision was the starting point for the miracle of the loaves and fish. Matthew 14:14 tells us, *"And when Jesus went out He **saw** a great multitude; and He was moved with compassion for them, and healed their sick"* (NKJV, emphasis added).

An additional insight into Jesus's vision is found in Mark's account of these events. He writes in Mark 6:33–34, *"They arrived before them and came together to Him. And Jesus, when He came out, **saw** a great multitude and was moved with compassion for them, because they were like sheep not having a shepherd"* (NKJV, emphasis added).

Both Matthew and Mark stress the centerpiece of Jesus's vision: compassion! He didn't just see them, He saw them and was moved with compassion for them. Remember, in the eyes of the disciples, the people were a bit of a problem. The crowd was an irritant that they wanted to send away in a hurry. But Jesus saw the crowd as sheep without a shepherd. He was concerned. He was attuned to their spiritual and physical needs. Their welfare mattered to Him. Their hunger and lostness touched His heart so deeply, He was moved with compassion to help and perform a miracle.

The word for compassion is the Greek word *splanchizo-mia*: "To have compassion, pity, or deep empathy." Literally, it describes one's bowels (your inner being) being moved with sympathy and pity toward others. It's gut-level love. You can't stop it. So herein lies the secret to re-visioning. When our vision aligns with Jesus we see through the lens of His heart and not our own. We then, like Him, are filled with compassion. And compassion is a powerful transforming force. God can use it.

In other words, when we see people as Jesus sees them, His compassion fills our heart to help. We passionately desire His divine assistance because we deeply care about those He has called us to serve, whether that is our family, our church, our neighbors, our mission field, our business, or so on. We momentarily place ourselves on the back burner and become engulfed in our passion to see God work for those who need His abundance.

But we have a problem. Our culture today is blinded by a thick swath of selfishness and busyness. It's hard for us to see like Jesus sees because we have so many layers to peel away—including our own selfish habits and motives that often become all wrapped up in our dreams of serving God or helping others. We all have a complex combination of reasons that we want to help people. Some are wonderful. Some are very selfish. And stripping away those vision-obstructing wrappings can be difficult. It takes a merciful work of God and our surrender.

Are you in need of some re-visioning? For me the major obstacle obstructing my vision for the people in our community was our need for a building. What's the object that is consuming *your* visual field right now? Is it a financial issue? A broken relationship? Perhaps it's a great bundle of needs that snowballed into a burden that has your knees buckling?

The good news is that you can choose to begin to see the way that Jesus does. I want to share with you three simple actions you can make to re-vision your life and dream and prepare to release a miracle. These are steps to surrender and commit to becoming a blessing maker.

How To Re-Vision

Re-visioning is something you and your Heavenly Father do together. It's not a solo act on God's part or yours. It is a process where God lovingly works with you to bring into focus what He wants you to see. Here's an example from my childhood: I was about nine years old. My dad and I were visiting one of his friends whose house was on a large lake. On his back patio his friend had a rustic-looking telescope. I remember my dad trying to get me to see a "tiny old house" through the telescope. But no matter how hard I looked, I couldn't see it. I got so frustrated, putting my eye to the lens again and again, to no avail.

Seeing my frustration, Dad looked through the telescope one more time. He carefully dialed in the location. "Look again," he said. I did. Nothing.

So, he took things into his own hands for a moment. He gently grabbed my little jaws and maneuvered my head and the telescope until they were in proper alignment. Then, all of a sudden, with his hands guiding me, *I saw it*. A tiny little house, miles away, sprang into focus. It looked like I could almost touch it.

That image of my dad and the telescope seems so much like what God does with us—and it's an encouragement. You see, not all the pressure for moving from blindness into new vision falls upon us. It would be hopeless if it did! Re-visioning is not a process we have to do alone. Jesus will help us! Why? He wants us to see things as He does. He is more eager to work miracles through your life than you are. His hands are on you already, and He is beginning to guide you to see things with heaven's focus. Let's let Him.

There are three things you can do to allow and accelerate God's re-visioning process in your life, moving away from blindness into His kind of sight, where dreams and miracles begin to really happen:

1. Decide to really see the people around you.

Yes, this is a choice. Seeing (truly seeing) others never just happens. It is easy to become so absorbed in the need that confronts us that we lose sight of the people we are called to love. This happens to the best of us.

I remember listening to a preacher telling about his trip to a diamond mine. As he watched the workers laboring, he became burdened for them, burdened to the point where he was overcome. As he stood at the top of one of the mounds of rock along the mine, he screamed out at the top of his lungs. "The rocks are not the diamonds," he cried. "The people are the diamonds!"

The people are the diamonds. What a powerful image.

To see the true value of the people around us, we have to be close enough to see them. We have to have the time, space, and willingness to allow God to move us until others come into focus. One of the decisions I made while writing this book was not to write it all in my office, but to write as much as I could while sitting in the café area of a local grocery store. It wasn't the most efficient in terms of "undivided" attention, but it kept me grounded and engaged with the point of this whole book. And, as seeing people does to you, my vision continued to change as I met new neighbors, had fresh conversations, and experienced the divine interruptions" that help us understand why miracles matter to God in the first place.

2. *Decide to really see the Scriptures.*

Guess what? This is a choice too. We all approach God's Word with lenses that filter out parts of it and put others into focus. We need to ask God to use His Spirit to guide us into a fuller view of the Bible.

Reading the Scriptures will help form your heart so your eyes see correctly. Jesus saw the people He was about to serve as sheep without a shepherd. Embedded within that description is Christ's incredible love for His sheep. His longing is to meet their needs and to be with them. Re-visioning requires that we see people as God sees them—the sheep Jesus died for. To see people with value has nothing to do with being a pastor or a clergy member. It has everything to do with being a follower of Jesus Christ and having His heart for people. If Jesus lives in you, the Shepherd of your soul wants to express His love for His other sheep through you.

Often, God uses practices to help us here. There is a classical practice for reading the Scripture called "*Lectio Divina*." It is a combination of reading, meditation, prayer, and contemplation. The goal is not to study the Bible with your head but with your heart, while trusting the Holy Spirit to help you grow in the knowledge of God's Word and in fellowship with Him.

3. Decide to really help people.

Re-vision is not only seeing but taking action. Many times we can see what God wants to do, and unfortunately it ends there. Re-visioning requires you to make the decision to step forward to help. Better stated—seeing is doing! Friend, you might not have a lot of resources to work with at the moment. However, the compassion that fills your heart for those God has placed around you will not permit you to do nothing. Make the choice now to do something—even if it seems like little or nothing. Remember, from Jesus's perspective, giving someone a cup of water is a powerful act of love.

Over a Hamburger

Through a series of unexpected (to us) events, Craigo's went into foreclosure. The property was going to be auctioned off by the city and the starting bid was $371,000.

In the midst of everything else going on for us at that time, our previous small A-frame church had been torched by an arsonist. A young man in the dark of a summer night, threw Molotov cocktails through the window into our sanctuary.

Flames erupted, consuming our sanctuary. But his act of destruction had remarkable unforeseen consequences.

From that shock and hardship, support poured in from the community we knew we had and the community we never imagined. We had monies from all over the world come in to help our church recover. It was truly God working. However, even with all the money we had managed to raise and the gifts and support from after the fire, we were short. $165,000 short. What we had was great, but it still wasn't enough.

Because of the fire, I had an odd opportunity to speak on a heavy metal radio station. (That was a trip!) However, an old college buddy, whom I hadn't spoken with in years, "happened" to be listening. He gave me a call and we reconnected. He was sad to hear what had happened to the church and wanted to know what he could do to help. Unfortunately, he didn't have $165,000 just laying around. But it was nice to know he cared.

Several weeks passed. My friend reached out again. "Hey Mark," he said. "I have a client who would like to meet you for lunch. Can you?" He didn't give a lot of information about the meeting, but mentioned that the man had heard what happened to our church and wanted to talk about it.

So we all met at Red Robin for a burger. During our lunch, this total stranger, a man I had never met before, asked me a question: "What is your vision for the building you want to buy?" I set my burger down and told him about Craigo's. "Our vision is to buy this store, which has been a cancer in our community for a long time. We want to transform it. We want to turn it into a place where lives can be changed. We want to help the struggling single mother. Help people in our neighborhood get off drugs. We want to serve and love our community. We want to show them Jesus."

I don't think this man was even a believer. But that didn't stop God. This man didn't blink an eye. Just listened. Then, he cleared his throat, and loaves (or burgers) seemed to multiply into miraculous provision. "I will put up the $165,000 for you," he said.

And he did. He gave the money. He paid all the attorney fees. He had his own lawyer negotiate for us at the auction. He filed all the paperwork. We got the building. We were *given* the building. God somehow turned the nothing we had into everything we needed. But it only happened after I began to reject my blindness and see things like He did. After I began to re-vision, Jesus waited until I embraced His dream before He began a miracle in the empty aisles of Craigo's. When it was clear to me what *His* vision was, and I embraced it with all my heart, then the full provision came.

Friend, can you see your vision changing? Is Jesus's heart for your situation coming into focus? If so, get ready. You're making a critical movement to open a door of divine possibilities. Miracles can happen. God's dream for you can begin to come true. You are a blessing maker.

Allow God to steer your sight, to focus your eyes on what He sees. Now that your eyes are changing, you're getting ready to move from scarcity to sufficiency.

Practice: *Lectio Divina*

Let me briefly explain the steps of the Lectio Divina practice mentioned above. This can help you with one of the key steps of re-visioning: truly seeing the Scriptures. Remember that focusing on the fullness of the Bible is one of the best ways to see like God sees!

- ### Step one: Read

Find a quiet place where you won't be disturbed and you can focus. Begin by reading through a chosen passage slowly several times. While doing so, ask yourself, *What's going on in this passage? What is it saying?*

- ### Step two: Meditate

Once you have determined what the passage is saying, engage in an unhurried process of thinking about what you just read. As you ponder, allow the Holy Spirit to speak to your heart. Try to see the passage as you think God would. Allow for time to let it soak in.

- ### Step three: Pray

Don't pray a scripted prayer, but pray from your heart. Allow your reading and meditation to shape your words toward God. You may have discovered a coldness of heart, or blinders, that has altered your vision. Here you can ask God to restore your heart and your sight. You can ask Him to help you see people as He sees them. Take time to focus the Bible back to God through your heart.

- *Step four: Contemplate*

This final step is where you fully listen to the voice of God. Allow Him to speak to you about Himself through this part of the Bible. Trust Him to show you how to apply what you have learned into your life's context. This is different from meditation above because it becomes focused on how the passage will connect with your life and walk with God.

Great passages for Lectio Divina: Ezekiel 34, Psalms 23, and John 10. (Don't try to work these passages all at once. Break each one up into bite-sized sections of a few verses that are right for the process. The goal is connecting in a new way with God through His Word, not just making it through a chunk of the Bible.)

A PRAYER FOR YOUR EYES

When you're ready, ask God to help you see the world like Jesus does:

Dear God, please touch my heart. Take away what blinds me. Allow the scales of my own needs, wishes, and wants to vanish. Fill my heart with your compassion, so that I can see people like you see them. Place your hands upon my face, and direct my vision today. When your sight comes into focus, fill my heart with peace and move me to action, so that the hearts of those who are hungry may see and experience what you have provided and prepared for them. Amen.

Chapter 3

Movement Two:
FROM SCARCITY
TO SUFFICIENCY

*When it was evening, His disciples came to Him,
saying, "This is a deserted place, and the hour is
already late. Send the multitudes away, that they
may go into the villages and buy themselves food."*
MATTHEW 14:15 (NKJV)

t was a breezy Puerto Rican night. Warm and beautiful. I had
just finished preaching an awesome message at a church service (at least I thought it was awesome) and was mingling with
a few hundred joyful people after the service, when I saw my
interpreter motioning for my attention. So I navigated through
the crowd toward him, noticing that he was standing with a
"sweet little grandma" type. I gave granny a big hug, greeting her
with my limited Spanish. Then the interpreter spoke up. "Pastor, she believes God has something He wants her to tell you!" I
perked up.

All ears and eager to hear, I leaned in close. I didn't want to miss a word. It was noisy as people were talking and beginning to exit the building. Kind of chaotic. I thought she was going to say something along the lines of, "God bless you, honey. Keep serving the Lord! I am praying for you."

Well, I was wrong. She began to speak in a quick, clipped Spanish. To make sure I understood every word in the loud room, the interpreter positioned his mouth about two inches from my ear, hands cupped like a megaphone, and shouted the translation at an ungodly decibel.

"Pastor!" I flinched a little. "The Lord told me to tell you, "YOU ARE THE PROBLEM!" There is so much more that God wants to do in your life, your family, your church, and your community, but YOU ARE THE PROBLEM!"

Not the word of encouragement I had expected. I wasn't prepared for it. Nor could I have guessed in a million years this sweet little granny would give me such a direct message.

"YOU ARE THE PROBLEM!" I was stunned. *Are you serious?* I thought. *How in the world could I be the problem? After all, I flew all the way from Oregon to share the gospel with you here in Puerto Rico. And I am the problem? Figure that!*

I would have never expected to hear those words. But what really troubled me was wondering if they were true.

Now, fast-forward several months. My family had been given a gift by several friends to go on a cruise for vacation. We had never been on a cruise before. We were ecstatic and thankful for their generosity. At the time, my children were ten, seven, and three, with one more "in the oven." On one particular afternoon of our trip, we were onboard ship sitting around a table talking church stuff with some of our pastor friends also on the cruise. Our kids were at the table too, enjoying hot dogs, fries, and plenty of a sugary orange-flavored drink. (Any parents reading this are beginning to cringe.) After enjoying our dining experience for a whole fifteen minutes, the inevitable started. The sugar hit their little bloodstreams, kicked childhood into high gear, and our floating dining disaster began.

The French fries became boats navigating down orange currents of soda streaming across the table. Ketchup and mustard packets were discovered to be serviceable ammunition as the kids found out that if they smashed a packet with their fist, the contents would streak across the table. Fun, huh?

Then, in addition to squirting ketchup and French fry boats, our youngest began to serenade our table with her signature hit single, "I Do Not Want to Take a Nap." By this time, my wife, who was six and a half months pregnant, gave a glare that informed me, *These are your kids!* Graciously I returned the look: *Ma'am, you are mistaken. I believe these are your children!*

In the middle of the chaos, I heard a voice. It was whispering gently those familiar (but forgotten by then) words in my heart and mind. *Pastor,* it said, *you are the problem.*

Whoa, I thought. *I'm in double trouble now. My kids have turned my wife against me, and a Bible-toting Puerto Rican grandmother is stalking me on my vacation.*

In the turmoil of that chaotic table, Jesus began to speak powerfully to my heart and mind. He made it explicitly clear to me that a critical movement needed to happen in my mind and thinking—if I was to be a blessing maker. A movement whereby a mentality of scarcity that had defined my life and ministry would be replaced. But replaced by what?

Beyond the Scarcity Mentality

A scarcity mentality is sometimes unnoticeable. Like me, you may not even recognize you have it. A scarcity mentality is a prohibitive way of thinking that restricts you from participating in a miracle that God has called you to be a part of. It paralyzes your mind and faith to the limitations of your own resources and factors out what God may want to do in the situation.

Friend, scarcity thinking will make us the problem in God's dream to bless others. God's desire is for His blessings to flow through our lives to reach others. He wants us to be an open pipeline for His blessings to flow through our lives to reach others. If our pipe is clogged by scarcity thinking, the blessing will not reach the ones who need it. Therefore, a movement in our thinking is necessary, from defining our lives by the scarcity that surrounds us, to seeing the perfect sufficiency that is ours through Jesus.

For that movement to happen, we have to understand the wrong mindset so we can change it. But you're probably asking, What exactly is a scarcity mentality, and how can I tell if it is affecting me? Let's answer that question with the help of Jesus and His disciples.

To feed or not to feed, that was the question. Jesus and His disciples saw the situation of the hungry crowd differently. Jesus knew that the massive number of people present had no bearing on the Father's ability to provide. He knew His Father was capable of providing for twenty thousand people as easily as He could for one. Jesus's mindset was that they could feed the people—for God is all sufficient!

The Father's ability to provide for His dream is not restricted by location or any lack of resources. God is all sufficient. All the time. In all places. Even on a beachfront with multitudes of hungry people clamoring for food. Even when the church is burning and Craigo's is $165,000 out of your reach. Even in *your* difficult situation—whatever it is. God can do what no one else can do. But He may be waiting on you.

A sufficiency mentality believes God is who He says He is and trusts Him to do what only He is capable of doing! Sufficiency says, "God is good, and there is enough." This is the way we ought to think. This is the truth about God the provider. But at times we find our thought processes resonating with the disciples, thinking that God must not really care about *this* need enough, and we are on our own with far too little to meet the need.

The disciples' thinking, like mine has often been and yours might be now, was out of tune. It was not aligned with Christ's understanding of the Father or of God's dream. They reasoned, "We can't feed them; send them away. There are too many people here to feed!" Their logic was grounded not in a sufficiency mentality, but a scarcity mentality. *A scarcity mentality is a prohibitive way of thinking. It is a denial. It prevents God's grace and provision from flowing through your life to bless others.*

A mindset of scarcity chains your heart, mind, and faith

to a reality that is confined to your own ability, experiences, logic, and resources. It limits what can be done to your power. It suffocates the notion that an infinite God may want to intervene in your finite circumstances. A scarcity mindset factors God out of the equation, either temporarily or permanently. It forces us to attempt to redefine or figure out a solution to resolve the problem ourselves. That's exactly what the disciples were doing when they told Jesus to send the people away in Matthew 14:15–17. Listen:

> *As evening approached, the disciples came to him and said, "This is a remote place, and it's already getting late. Send the crowds away, so they can go to the villages and buy themselves some food."*
>
> *Jesus replied, "They do not need to go away. You give them something to eat."*
>
> *"We have here only five loaves of bread and two fish," they answered.* (NIV)

In all honesty, I probably would have made a similar request to Jesus. They care. They are trying to stay one step ahead of a needy crowd whose blood-sugar levels are dropping rapidly. (Sometimes just trying to figure out what's for dinner in our household of six is nerve-racking. So there's no way I'm going to judge Jesus's boys for trying to get out of feeding 15,000–20,000 people.) And what did their resources consist of? A sack lunch for a kid. These few loaves of bread were not twenty-four inch baguettes, nor were the fish two fifteen-pound salmon. I have two sons, Micah and Myles. For dinner, if all they had on their plate were two sardine-sized fish and a few rolls, I know what their response would be. "Dad, where is the *real* dinner?"

These verses reveal the heart of the scarcity mindset—focusing on a God-less solution to a problem God longs to solve. Scarcity thinking has the potential to stop us from doing our part to join God's dream. It can prevent us from allowing God to change our nothing into something and our something into everything. It can cause us to miss our part in God's dream.

But there's hope—you and I can uncover our own areas of scarcity thinking and give them to God. Once we understand where we think this way, God can help us reboot our mindset to be in harmony with His dream.

Here are some of the focused areas that are notorious for shaping within us a scarcity mindset.

Wrong Focus Area #1—The Remoteness of the place (How far away help is).

Like Pastor Chester in the story that began this book, have you ever been stuck in the "middle of nowhere"? That's how it feels to be faced with a need you cannot meet. In Matthew 14:15, the disciples tell Jesus that they are in a remote place. This is the lie that because of where we are, there aren't options. They are too far away.

So many times when we are faced with a great need, we think that other grass looks greener. That's what the disciples were thinking. But the truth of the matter is, God didn't place you in greener grasses—he placed you here. Yes, here. The place of need, not the place of obvious provision.

We are exactly where He wants us to be, even when we can't see how our situation is going to work out.

Isn't it funny how the disciples are informing Jesus of their whereabouts, as if He is unaware of their surroundings. You can almost hear the sarcasm. "Umm, Jesus, you may have been too busy preaching to notice, but *WE ARE IN THE MIDDLE OF NOWHERE.*"

But Jesus is totally aware of their location. (After all, He made it!) He is also aware of your location. He knows exactly where we are, not only geographically, but emotionally, spiritually, financially. Every "where" we may find ourselves, He knows. He is there.

What the disciples failed to realize is the same issue that we all need to face. The issue of our need is not where we are, but where God is. God is omnipresent—meaning He is everywhere! For you and me, this should encourage our hearts, because no matter how remote the place is where we are—God is present! So to tune, turn the thought-peg of your mind until you hear a note in perfect pitch, ringing out, *"It's not about where I am, but where God is—because where He is all things are possible!"*

Wrong Focus Area #2—How late it is.

Another sour note affecting the disciples' thinking was their focus on time. This is the lie that it is "too late" for God to do anything. The disciples deemed it their duty to inform Jesus of the lateness of the hour. A scarcity mentality obsesses over limitations of time. It seems to believe that God is required to move within a certain timeframe.

When you and I are in need, our tendency is to wonder why God is taking His own sweet time to help. We stress and panic because we feel that with each tick of the clock, all hope is running out. But God is not limited by time! *We* are the ones who live inside the limitations of time, not God. He exists outside of time! He is the eternal God, and He is not in a hurry. Like the older folk in our church say, "He may not come when you want Him, but He's always right on time!"

Once, my friend Don and his wife, Marlene, were serving as pastors in a small church. They had received a much-needed check in the mail for $500. Like Jonah was overjoyed for the plant the Lord had prepared for him on a scorching hot day, Don and Marlene were overjoyed for that check. However, in the midst of their joy the Lord spoke to Don and told him to give a new pastor that was coming to serve in a nearby town $300 dollars of the money. So, being obedient to that leading, Don and his wife went to bless the pastor.

When they arrived at the church, they asked a lady in the church of the pastor's whereabouts. She informed them that he never showed up. Don and his wife were puzzled because they were sure the Lord had instructed them to give $300 to this pastor. They drove home perplexed, the money still in their pocket.

Months later, Don bumped into a friend from the same area. He asked about the pastor they believed they were to give the money to. The friend informed him the man was living on the coast somewhere. Why? The word was, because he had $300 in debt, and he believed he couldn't pay it off if he became a pastor.

God had not forgotten this prospective pastor; he was just on a different time schedule. This pastor's provision was on the way. God was faithful to send what was needed, but the man failed to wait for it to come.

How many times might we have missed the full provision of God because of our fear and impatience?

Wrong Focus Area #3—Why we should send people somewhere else.

This is the lie that people will be better served elsewhere, rather than in the place of need. This is the belief that prompted the disciples' request for Jesus to send the crowd away so they could find food. As you'll discover shortly God's heartbeat *is:* If He can get it through you, He will get it to you. Sending people away is the antithesis of what God wants to do. He wants to provide *here*. He provided for the crowd in a place the disciples never imagined. And He is right here where you are now; He can do the same for you!

The temptation to send others away is real, though. And it is based in our desire for their good. After all, it's "realistic" to point someone away from here if what they need is nowhere in sight. People in need can become a burden. They can get on your nerves at times.

I was talking with my friend Teddy who was telling me about a man ("Johnny") who had been a nuisance for a number of years in his life. From his perspective, Johnny could have been a regular on a bad reality show. You've heard the story before: bad choices, bad drug abuse, bad company, and so on.

For years Teddy spent time talking with him about life

and the Lord. After a few years of futile conversation, Teddy was ready to send Johnny away. Johnny's justification of his lifestyle and behavior became harder and harder for Teddy to stomach. He said it got to the point he wanted nothing to do with the guy at all—he wanted to send him away. But he didn't.

One morning Teddy was lying on his bed, and for some odd reason started to think about Johnny. *That guy is never going to change*, he thought. But God works in remarkable ways.

That same day he saw Johnny at the store, and he was a changed man! Teddy said Johnny went on to tell him how the Lord had been changing his life, and he thanked Teddy for all those times he talked and prayed with him. The transformation in his life was amazing. My buddy Teddy was so happy he had not sent Johnny away. Where would Johnny be today if he had done so? Johnny became a devoted follower of Christ who is now being used as a pipeline by God to bless the lives of others.

Wrong Focus Area #4—What we do not have.

When Jesus told the disciples to give the people something to eat, they responded by saying, "All we have here are five loaves and two fish." They were in essence telling Jesus, "What we have in our possession is absolutely nothing in comparison to what's needed to feed this crowd."

Isn't it interesting, though. While the focus of their words is on what they *have*, the *point* of their words is on what they don't. Their response to Jesus's question emphasized the inadequacy of their resource. They minimized an impossibly small gift because of the massive need it could not possibly fill. Their attention was on what they didn't have, not what they did have.

Sound familiar? This is the temptation we face constantly as well. And who would blame us? After all, it's just common sense.

But heaven's common sense isn't our own. And in fact, God rarely calls us to a task we are fully prepared to do. His call dwarfs our own abilities and resources. That's part of the point of it. The temptation to focus on the "don't have" is strong. However, if our focus is solely on the need, a scarcity mindset will develop. And like me, you may find yourself becoming the problem.

What is it you're focusing on right now? What is the resounding need that is clamoring for all your attention and energy? What is the void that is slowly moving you into a way of thinking, closing you in and shutting God out? Is it a need in your job, your ministry, your family, your community? No matter what the size of the troubling issue is, tune it out and focus on the thing Jesus is drawing to your attention. Look at the meal, even if it is tiny. Don't stare at the ten thousand empty plates.

Remember this incredible verse:

And my God shall supply all your need according to His riches in glory by Christ Jesus. Now to our God and Father be glory forever and ever. Amen. (Phil. 4:19–20, NKJV)

Moving My Mindset

Now back to the ship. Prior to God speaking to my heart through the unexpected message in Puerto Rico, and its haunting return to my mind on the ship, I would have never thought I was the problem. I didn't see that I needed a movement in my thinking. After all, I prayed and read my Bible faithfully. I trusted the Lord with all my heart to meet all my needs. I really did.

So then, why was I still frustrated in trying to accomplish what God had placed in my heart? Honestly, I had no idea that my thinking could impact God's ability to turn nothing into something and something into everything. But it could, and it did. Our faith cannot demand anything of God that is not in His will for our lives. But He often chooses to not release His provision without it.

I never will forget the moment on the cruise when God reminded me I was the problem. In that instant, a movement took place in my thinking. Right there in the midst of the chaos at the table. In my heart, I said, "Lord, forgive me for my scarcity mindset. And with your help I will no longer be the problem." In that instant, a peaceful movement took place in my mindset and in my heart. A fresh hope blossomed in my soul. I felt as if the handcuffs I had placed on God were broken, and I had a new confidence that God could do great things despite my circumstances. I could get a radiant glimpse of His dream for my life and our church.

Friend, chances are you are not in Puerto Rico, nor on a ship trying to eat a meal surrounded by three hyperactive kids. However, you are in a place right now where the Holy Spirit can reach you and speak to your heart. Take a moment and ask the Lord if your thinking is in need of adjustment. He is faithful and will let you know yea or nay. If He says no, great! If He says yes, repentance is in order. Quietly tell Him you are sorry and ask Him to remove your scarcity mindset. He will be glad to do it, and you will be overjoyed He did! And you will find yourself thinking like the blessing maker Jesus wants you to be.

PRAYER OF REPENTANCE

Jesus, forgive me. I'm so sorry for the way I have been thinking. Forgive me for the times that the thoughts in my heart and mind have prevented you from working through me. I'm guilty of having a scarcity mindset. Wash me and change my thinking. Please give me a sufficiency mindset. I no longer want to be the problem. I want to be a part of your answer, your solution. Amen.

Chapter 4

Movement Three:

FROM OFFBEAT TO ONBEAT

But Jesus said to them,
"They do not need to go away.
You give them something to eat."

MATTHEW 14:16 (NKJV)

Have you ever found yourself tapping your foot while listening to the beat of a song playing in your favorite restaurant? Are you guilty of doing the "bobble-head" to the beat of the bass blasting on iTunes or Pandora? Has a classical piece graced your ears, to send your body swaying to the swelling of the thundering timpani? Or have you ever rocked to the pulse of a subwoofer blowing you away with a heavy hip-hop beat?

Of course you have. We all have been moved a time or two by an external beat.

When God made you, He wired you for sound. He made you to hear it, feel it, to be emotionally and physically moved by it. In fact, He gave you a metronome in the center of your chest that beats in rhythm to keep you alive—it's called your heart.

A dream requires a beat—the very heartbeat of God! God's heartbeat pounds with His love and passion for all people. It throbs to show His goodness and mercy to those around you, while also longing to use your life in ways that will amaze you and others. His heart yearns to fulfill the dream of His heart by taking the nothing that you have and making it everything, so that the world will be blessed and know Him personally and intimately.

The challenge you and I face today is that our culture and world are filled with many distracting beats. While many of these beats are "catchy," they compete with God's heartbeat. These competing rhythms pulsate to make us focus solely on ourselves. There are shallow and quick impulses that lack vibration of eternity. They're short-lived and, in the long run, very unfulfilling and unsatisfying. If we become absorbed in their groove, our hearts will not beat to serve others and fulfill God's dream. Therefore a movement is needed for us to move from the world and our cultures that are offbeat to God's heartbeat.

For this to happen, a movement is necessary! A movement that requires you and I to sync our heartbeat with His. It's important for us to understand that God's heart pulsates with divine purpose. When our hearts are in sync with the Father's heart, we are connected to His purpose. This connection releases Him to allow miracles and blessing to gush through our lives for His glory and His purpose. But the question is, *"What is His purpose—and how can I hear His heartbeat?"*

To answer the question, I'll loan you a stethoscope. In one ear you're going to hear about a race, and in the other ear you're going to listen once again to the Matthew 14 passage.

In a few moments, you're going to hear God's heartbeat loud and clear, with the goal of helping your heart and mine to sync up with His.

From Start to Finish

My oldest son is a gifted sprinter. One of the races he ran throughout his high school and college track career was the 4 x 1 relay. The 4 x 1 is a 400-meter sprint where four guys each run a 100-meter leg with a baton in hand. When the gun sounds, the first man is out of the blocks; he runs and then passes the baton to the second runner. The second runner then sprints 100 meters and passes the baton to the third runner. The third runner sprints and finally passes the baton to the anchor leg, who then flies to the finish line.

During this brief race, what worries the coaches, runners, and spectators are the handoffs with the baton. Seamless and good handoffs are the name of the game. If any runner drops the baton, they lose the race. If a handoff is made outside the allotted space, they lose the race. If a person fails to hand off the baton, they lose the race. For the team to win the race they not only have to run fast, but the baton must reach the destination—the finish line.

Now let's turn our attention to the other ear. While you're listening, allow your eyes to follow along, focusing on the baton-like movements of the five loaves and the two fish in Matthew 14:18–19. Watch and listen closely as the dream of God unfolds.

"Bring them here to me," he said. And he directed the

people to sit down on the grass. Taking the five loave and the two fish and looking up to heaven, he gave thanks and broke the loaves. Then he gave them to the disciples, and the disciples gave them to the people. (Matt. 14:18–19, NIV)

Through these few insightful lines, we see the morsels of nothing moving from hand to hand until they reach the finish line—*the people.* The progression went like this:

- *The little boy gave the lunch to the disciples.*
- *The disciples gave the lunch to Jesus.*
- *Jesus gave the lunch to the Father.*
- *Jesus gave the lunch back to the disciples.*
- *The disciples gave the lunch to the people.*
- *The disciples picked up the leftovers.*

From this brief sound bite we can safely conclude that no person involved in the relay (Jesus, the little boy, the disciples) became self-serving. They all faithfully relayed the provision until the bread and fish reached the people who needed it. No one aborted the process because they knew Jesus's intention— the Father's purpose. His heartbeat was to bless the people!

Did you hear it?

If so, you did better than I did for years. I read this passage dozens of times. I could have easily told you with my eyes closed how the bread and fish passed through holy hands to hungry mouths. However, it wasn't until the Lord opened my ears in prayer that I heard His heartbeat pounding in my soul saying,

If I can get it through you, I can get it to you!
In other words,

If God can get His provisions (blessings, wisdom, finances, strength, etc.) through you, He will place what you need in your hands and bless it, so that you will have everything you need to serve the person or persons He desires to bless.

I want to give you a word of caution here. Don't be fooled. This is not simply some catchy saying. A formula to twist God's arm. It is a truth that is fleshed out throughout the entire Bible. God uses people who obey Him. And when you and I are obedient to Him, He is able to work through our lives in remarkable ways. There is a depth in these two phrases that, once grasped, will move your heart to a miracle.

To You and Through You

We live in a consumer society. Everywhere you turn there is something for sale, something bigger, brighter, and better; something you're told you "need." The thirst for more is a temptation we all face.

But this is deeply troubling. A heart that beats for purely selfish consumption is full in the wrong ways, full with the wrong things. It's not experiencing its own emptiness. And so, it will never experience the miracle of nothing becoming everything. Consumption can never provide for us. In a divine paradox, it is our emptiness that begins to allow us to experience God's fullness.

What would have happened if the hungry disciples decided themselves to eat the meager bread and fish? The answer is easy. There would have been no miracle. They would have nullified the process by self-consumption. Sure, they might have appeased their hunger a bit, but the other 14,999–19,999 people would have been left hungering.

I feel it's important to say this here: The acquisition of material stuff is not the miracle of what nothing becoming something, and something becoming everything is about. Many people have the ability to acquire stuff, and it takes no miracle to make it happen. Some people are like the rich man in the Bible, who had barns of stuff, but there was no redemptive value in what he possessed, because he was a 100 percent self-consumer. It was all for him and no one else. And for a quick note, God is not going to anoint a person whose heartbeat is selfishness, because it lacks a critical component—others!

Don't get me wrong, God does bless people with material means, and folks that have been blessed by God in that fashion should not feel guilty, nor should they be condemned by others. God is concerned about your needs and mine. And He is faithful to meet our needs. We will discuss more about that later; however, for now, what's important is that your heart syncs with His. That will make sure our treasure is really in the right place!

To you and through you operates on an entirely different premise than what is mentioned above. When your heartbeat syncs with God's heartbeat, you change. *You become a distributor and not a consumer!* You are carrying the baton and passing it so it reaches the finish line (others). You are a part of a great team that relays the blessings of God to a broken and hungry world. You are passionate about being generous and faithful. With all your heart, you make sure you give to others what God desires, so He can eternally impact the ones who receive His blessing from your hand.

A Brown Envelope

It had been a rough summer. I was a junior in college, living in my parents' house, with no summer job. This was hard on me. Every summer I always worked to help offset my expenses for school. No summer work meant I would have even more difficulty paying for books and tuition when classes started. But for whatever reason, despite my best efforts, I could not land a job. However, after weeks of endless searching, I felt in my heart that God wanted me to spend the rest of my summer in prayer and study and sharing my faith with people on the street. Sounds pretty spiritual, huh? Maybe, but it wasn't going to pay any of my bills.

My joblessness provoked from my dad what my brothers and I called the "Parasite Speech." I don't think he was even serious when he gave it because it would take all he could muster to keep from laughing. It began with the familiar rhetorical question, "Do you know what a parasite is?" to which I would mumble some unintelligible syllables. Then he would proceed to educate me. He would say, "A parasite lives on a host and sucks it dry. That's what you and your brothers are doing to me—you guys are like parasites." My dad has given some good speeches in his life, but this was not one of my favorites. Joking or not.

Complicating matters, I had radically committed my life to Jesus Christ, and every other person in the house at the time, with the exception of my mother, thought I was off my rocker.

If that wasn't enough, I had pressure from my extended family, too. I can laugh at some of the trials I endured now, but at the time it wasn't a laughing matter! Those persecutions were no fun, and neither was my Parasitic Summer. My dad didn't charge me rent, but I always wanted to contribute something to him and my mother.

Time was running short—it was a week before classes were to resume, still no job, and still no money! What in the world was I going to do? So one morning when everyone was out of the house, I fell to my knees and cried out to the Lord. My heart was anxious, and all the pressure I was dealing with throughout the summer was coming to a head. While in prayer, I heard the mail carrier drop the mail through the slot in the front door. I stopped praying for a second and went to pick up the mail from the floor.

As I reached down to pick up the scattered letters, I noticed a small brown package with my name on it. The odd thing about the package was there was no return address or any indication of who sent it. When I opened the packet all that was present was a little note that said, *"Mark, this money is legit, God bless you from your Heavenly Father—Jehovah Jireh."*

I reached my hand further into the package and pulled out a single one-hundred-dollar bill. I reached in again and pulled out another. Finally, I tore the package open and pulled out a stack of fifty hundred dollar bills. I jumped so high with excitement and joy, I could have won a tip-off against Shaq! I stood there looking at the cash on my couch, and I couldn't believe it.

I thought to myself, "I have enough money to buy a small car to drive around town. I have money to buy books and pay for my tuition. Not only that, I can afford to splurge and buy a few extra burgers."

However, the Lord began to speak to my heart... *Mark, this is not all yours to keep.*

So, I called my dad and told him what had happened, to which he replied, "Boy, don't play like that!" Then he said, "I'll call you back," and he hung up the phone. About two minutes later he called back and asked, "Now, what happened?" I told him the whole story and then let him know I was going to give him $2000. And that's what I did, I gave him $2000, gave my tithe to the church, and gave hundred dollar bills to my immediate and extended family and a few other people. After I finished my giving spree, I had enough money to pay for my fall term at Portland State University, which was about $900.

You see, God did not give me that money to consume it on myself. HE GAVE IT TO ME TO GET IT THROUGH ME! I had been praying diligently for God to touch my family and draw them to Him. I had been praying for my community to be touched by Christ. He gave the money to me to get it through me! That event was a God showing for my immediate family, extended family, and our community. God used the provision of that $5,000 dollars to open a door for me to share Christ with my family in a powerful way. He wonderfully captured their attention and open their hearts more than ever before. As a result, many members of my family were strengthened in their faith, and others moved closer to following Jesus. Also, the persecution ended—my dad shut it down. I could now pray in peace without all my brother's shenanigans. My grandfather also affirmed me by telling me, *"Boy, just keep on doing what you're doing!"*

Also, news about what happened spread like wildfire throughout our community! I was invited to share the testimony of what happened in several of the leading churches in our community. And thereby spoke to hundreds of people. The $5,000 was great, but God's intention was to bless far more people than I could have imagined. What He did was fund an evangelistic burden I had as a twenty-one-year-old young man to reach my family and community with the gospel of Jesus Christ.

So you see, *To You and Through You* is not just some slick slogan. Nor is it all about cash! It is about God releasing through your life what is needed to change lives.

Are you ready to sync your heartbeat with God's? If so, simply give God the permission to flood your heart with His purpose. He will joyfully do that! By His grace make the resolve within your soul to be a distributor. Determine you will be a blessing maker. Purpose that what God gives to you, you will be faithful to make sure it reaches His intended destination. And finally, take the time to discover the extraordinary gift He has blessed, which is the vehicle for beautiful miracles to happen all around you.

Just think, the disciples had no idea how extraordinary the gift of the five loaves and two fish would become. It never crossed their mind how Jesus viewed their "nothingness," let alone what He planned to do with it. Maybe you are wondering, how does God see the little I have in my possession? And, better yet, what is He planning to do with it? Friend, in this next movement you are about to find some answers to those questions—some very encouraging answers!

A WORD OF PRAISE

O God, I praise you for your loud life-giving heartbeat. I praise you that at this very moment the rhythm of your heart is pounding in my chest. Thank you that you can get it to me, because you daily give me the grace to get it through me. Jesus, I appreciate that wonderful privilege. May you be ever glorified.

Chapter 5

Movement Four:
FROM ORDINARY TO
EXTRAORDINARY

"We have here only five loaves
of bread and two fish."
MATTHEW 14:17 (NIV)

Have you ever eaten a peanut butter and jelly sandwich? Have you ever sunk your teeth into a Reese's Peanut Butter Cup? Or, if you are a peanut butter junkie like me, have you ever smothered a graham cracker with mounds of the gooey stuff, and dunked it straight into a cold glass of milk? What a delicacy—huh! However, did you know, there is more to a peanut than just peanut butter? Way more! In fact, the little peanut which can be seen as "nothing" became something that helped many people.

In the 1800s the major cash crop in the South was cotton. Cotton was the lifeline of the economy and southern life. However, over-dependence on cotton had depleted the soil, and the crops were being destroyed by the boll weevil as well. There was desperate need for an agricultural next step to avert a looming economic crisis that would socially and economically hurt an already fragile South in the years during Reconstruction.

Enter George Washington Carver and God. Carver was a famed African-American scientist. The breadth and scope of his work was very extensive, including disciplines such as agriculture, botany, education, art, and invention. He tirelessly spent his life working with God using the gifts he was given to better the lives of people. He saw himself as a person whom God could get something to and through to bless the lives of needy people around him. As he would say, his purpose was to help the man who was "the farthest down."

One of the most famous stories about his life centers around a life-changing prayer he offered to God. "Lord," he prayed once, "show me all the mysteries of the universe." God's response to his heart was, *Your mind is too small to perceive that!* Following that experience, Dr. Carver then asked the Lord to show him all the mysteries of an ordinary peanut. A request that God granted him! During his lifetime, Dr. Carver invented over 300 products from an ordinary peanut, including dyes, paints, cooking oil, just to name a few.

Extraordinary. But here's the irony. Like Dr. Carver, many times to address a massive need we believe we need the universe to do so. We feel most of the time a big problem requires a big resource. God, on the other hand, says all you and I need is a measly peanut, or five loaves and two fish, in order to accomplish our vision or dream. While we pray for the far off, God is sometimes providing with what is right under our noses.

I get it! We struggle with the notion of nothing becoming everything because it smacks our natural process of reasoning right in the gut. But the truth of the matter is, God's miraculous provision can happen, has happened, and will happen. Remember insufficient resources and provisions are the stuff God uses to fuel His dreams. What we have to keep in mind is that God's ways are higher than our ways and His thoughts are higher than our thoughts—and sometimes, like in the case of Carver and the peanut, "higher" really means "humbler." His intentions go far deeper than you and I having enough money, bread, fish, or whatever it is you need. There's so much more He desires to accomplish in your life and in the lives of those you love. And what seems to us to be ordinary or even nothing, has great value in God's sight!

Your ordinary gift (what we consider to be nothing) is a power vehicle that God delights in using. It is an extraordinary gift of grace that provides an opportunity for God to "SHOW" and you to "GROW!" The problem with our ordinary gift is sometimes it becomes so commonplace to us—it's unnoticeable, or unidentifiable.

An Extraordinary Gift

Now ask yourself, *"What ordinary gift do I have?"* Maybe it is an idea or a deep passion of your heart? Could it be a small amount of money or some other overlooked item like Chester's simple song in the story that started this book? Or is it something small like Dr. Carver's peanut?

Regardless, it is an extraordinary gift from God, an extraordinary gift that allows Him the opportunity to do an amazing work in you and through you. God's intent is to use what is absolutely insufficient in our lives as a magnifier to make Himself known to us and the world. It is through the lens of our insufficiency God shows the world who He is and allows you and I to grow in our relationship with Him. Amazingly, He uses our nothing to accomplish His own unique purposes in our lives and the lives of others.

God's Primary Purpose

God wants real relationship with each of us. He passionately desires everyone to know Him intimately as Father and friend. Throughout the history of humankind, in pursuit of relationship, God has revealed Himself to seekers. Lovingly and faithfully He penetrates the darkness that veils the human soul. And in the light of His revelation He says to the seeing and hearing heart, *"I love you and I am here for you!"* In your sphere of life—your family, your church, your school, your job, your neighborhood, your business—there are people God is pursuing, people He is seeking to bring into the primary relationship they were created to experience.

Our insufficiencies provide a perfect stage for God to display His love and His purpose. In the center of this stage, He orchestrates redemptive miracles and blessings that show the world not only what He can do, but also who He is! *God stands on the stage of our nothing, so He can reveal Himself to those He loves as everything.*

Though the context is the preaching of the cross of Christ, 1 Corinthians 1:26–29 beautifully illustrates the *nothing* God uses for His stage. What He chose, I wouldn't have picked.

The Scripture reads,

> *Brothers and sisters, think of what you were when you were called. Not many of you were wise by human standards; not many were influential; not many were of noble birth. But God chose the foolish things of the world to shame the wise; God chose the weak things of the world to shame the strong. God chose the lowly things of this world and the despised things—and the things that are not—to nullify the things that are, so that no one may boast before him.* (NIV)

Paul is saying here, what the world calls foolish, weak, or nothing are the very things God chooses and uses to accomplish His plan. The "nothing stuff" is the wood that comprises the stage God stands on and works through to reveal Himself to our own hearts and the world around us. How beautiful and encouraging.

But there's another aspect of how God works that will encourage you even more!

Creative Control

God is a creative genius! Look at the world we live in, the topography, the different bodies of waters, color schemes, all the different types of trees, plants, animals, and the list goes on. As the Creator, God did some of His best work on a canvas of absolutely nothing. Genesis 1:1–2 says,

> *"In the beginning God created the heavens and the earth. Now the earth was formless and empty, darkness was over*

the surface of the deep, and the Spirit of God was hovering over the waters" (NIV).

These descriptive words describe an existing void in which there was nothing present until God acted and created.

There is a phrase theologians use to describe this creative act of God called, *creatio ex nihilo.* The term is Latin, meaning, "creation out of nothing." The term explains how the galaxies, the sun and the moon and the earth as we know it were formed and shaped not out of existing matter or substance, but solely by the activity of God. His powerful creative word alone. It's amazing to think, God took nothing and made the warmth of the sun, the cool mid-day breeze, fragrance of flowers, and all the beauty we enjoy on a daily basis!

To bring it closer to home and make it more mind-boggling, the God who made the massive universe out of nothing and chaos is equally concerned with the minutia of our lives. He knows our deepest needs and concerns and will meet those needs in very creative ways that will glorify Him! Even if that means creating a massive feast out of nothing like five loaves and two fish.

Before I became the lead pastor of Life Change Church, I used to visit a church in our community called Maranatha. Though Maranatha was not my home church, I was there so much everybody thought it was. One Sunday night while visiting, they had a mission service, where a small team was giving a report from their recent trip to Haiti. That night the pastor gave each member of the short-term mission team about five minutes to share his or her experience.

A woman in her early thirties took the mic and began to shout, *"Hallelujah, God is so good!"* She was so overcome with emotion that she could hardly talk. Finally, after several glances upward and shaking her head back and forth in awe of God's goodness, her words began to flow.

She explained with words filled with awe about how one of her jobs for the outreaches was to be the "Bread-Roll Distributor." All she was expected to do was give a roll to each person who asked and tell them, "God bless you!" When the rolls were all gone, that part of her job was finished. Easy enough!

So that morning she took her sack filled with several dozen rolls, slung it over her back, and started her day, not expecting the outcome. Excited to serve, she reached into the bag, and gave the rolls one by one to adults and children—blessing them.

Time flew by, and then it hit her, *"We've been here for a few hours, and I have given away so many rolls, this bag should be empty!"* She stood amazed—the bag was still bursting full! This realization made her a bit fearful to the point that she didn't dare look in the bag to see what was going on. So she decided to just keep handing out the rolls as long as she could. The team continued to minister for a few more hours, and when they finished she still had a bag full of bread rolls.

With the sack over her shoulder she went back to her room and emptied the bag on her bed. For the first time that day, the bag was completely empty, but her heart was completely full!

I was so impacted by her story. I'll never forget it. When you and I have everything we need all the time, we are prone to restrict the creative activity of God.

Dependency

The extraordinary gift of nothing aggressively challenges our natural tendency to live independent from God. Having "not enough," whether it's an issue of wisdom, health, money, or any other need, will gracefully maneuver us into a place of submission. It's in that place where we learn to become more dependent on God and less dependent on ourselves.

Logical reasoning subtly says, no God creativity required here—everything I need is already in the bank! The problem with that is, when you and I have a low dose of God, we will have an overdose of "I." Too much "I" is toxic and deadly! Having the extraordinary gift of nothing helps us with that dilemma. It forces us to have high doses of God's creative activity and a very low dose of *"self-sufficiency."* It forges within us what God wants for our lives and is essential for our spiritual growth and relationship with God—dependency.

Jesus says in John 5:19, *"Very truly I tell you, the Son can do nothing by himself; he can do only what he sees his Father doing, because whatever the Father does the Son also does"* (NIV).

Dependency is trusting God to be the ultimate source for your life. Jesus said He couldn't do anything without the Father. Neither can you or I. Sure we can be active and be busy people, but if our lives are going build the kingdom, the King must be our source! By His grace we learn to rely on Him and trust Him every day and in every moment to provide what we need for our journey. Like the old song goes,

Without God, I could do nothing, without him I would fail.
Without God, I would be drifting, like a ship with out a sail.

78

Dependency leads to obedience. Jesus said, "I only do what I see the Father doing." Through obedience, we learn to live our lives in sync with God's motions and movements. Our obedience is not a forced obligatory duty, but a worshipful response out of a loving heart for the Father and a knowledge of our need. We obey Him because we love, and the deepest passion of our heart is to live a life pleasing to Him. Therefore, we delight to say what He tells us, and to do what He shows us.

Also, dependency is two-way trust. Yes, we trust God to be our source, however, God also trusts us too. Just as God the Father trusted Jesus the Son to fulfill His purpose and will, He trusts us. See, dependency is partnership with you and God! The nothing He has placed in your hand is His investment that says to you, "I trust you!" I trust you to work with me so that my kingdom will come on earth as it is in heaven. Succinctly, what God and you have formed is a loving partnership. A partnership allows the spotlight to shine on the one who deserves it—God!

God's Glory

Matthew 5:16 says, *"In the same way, let your light shine before others, that they may see your good deeds and glorify your Father in heaven"* (NIV). When it's all said and done, the only thing we want anyone to say is, "God did that!" Just like there was no way the disciples could take credit for feeding the five thousand, we can't puff out our chests when God multiplies our fragments of nothing into something. Yes, we were a part of the process, but He is the one who created the miracle. He is the one who gets all the credit, and the glory!

Our works were just signs waving in the air, saying, "Look at God!"

See, when God is glorified, lives are transformed. When God is glorified, human brokenness is mended. When God is glorified, the forces of darkness are pushed back and captives are set free. When God is glorified, Jesus Christ is exalted and redemption becomes a reality in the hearts and souls of men and women.

I remember hearing former Free Methodist Bishop Robert Andrews speaking at a conference. The message he spoke that day greatly impacted me. His message focused on the *gory* and the *glory*. He expounded on how the world magnifies the gory and how the gory is an inescapable part of our human landscape. With tears in his eyes he began to weep as he proclaimed how God desires to overcome the gory of the world with his glory. When God's glory is present, he said (paraphrased), the broken of humanity can experience the loving touch of heaven and the sinful narrative can be changed to one of redemption. Amen!

Let's retrace our steps thus far on our journey to become blessing makers. The necessary movements we have talked about so far are movements we must make within ourselves. Beginning with moving from our dream to God's mind-blowing dream. His amazing dream that exceeds anything we could imagine. We then adjusted our eyesight with a bit of re-visioning, so we could focus on what matters to God the most—people!

Next we gladly moved away from being the problem to being a part of God's answer, by getting rid of scarcity mentality, and embracing one of sufficiency. Finally, we delved into the heart of the matter by finding God's heartbeat, which is: God wants to get His blessings to you so that He can get them through you. These are all powerful, life-changing movements that are moving you closer to being a blessing maker. The movements (movements without) we'll discuss in the following chapters will equip you in practical ways to do what is at this very moment stirring within your heart. By the time you finish reading , you'll have what you need to see your nothing become something, and your something become everything. You will be a blessing maker!

But for now, back to the gift at hand.

My friend right now at this very moment you have an extraordinary gift in your possession. A gift that God desires to use mightily for His purposes! However, I have a question for you. Do you know what that gift is, or have you overlooked it? Is so, no problem—that is about to change!

In the next few pages you're going identify your gift. And if I can let you in on a secret, you are going to be amazed what God is going to do with what you are about to discover!

A MOMENT OF REFLECTION

Ask yourself the question, "Do I value what God has given to me?" Be honest with your answer. If you do, thank God for it. If not, search your heart and discern with God's help the reason why and ask, what about your perspective do you need to change?

PART TWO

MOVEMENTS WITHOUT

Chapter 6

Movement Five:
FROM NOTHING TO SOMETHING

*We have here only five loaves of bread
and two fish.*

MATTHEW 14:17 (NIV)

With tears cascading down her face Lisa explained her predicament. When she came to church that morning all she had in her purse was a dollar and some change. She was distraught because she had no money to give the Lord. Quickly, I tried to persuade her to think otherwise, because she is a faithful follower of Jesus who serves Him with a passionate heart. I told her, *"Money is only one thing you can give to the Lord, but it is not the only thing. There is a lot more to give to Jesus than money!"* She was also worried because a new school week was beginning, and she didn't have lunch money to give to her sons for the week. She was a single mother, and things for her that month had gotten extremely tight. When she told me her problem, my heart went out to her. However, at that moment I didn't have a single cent in my pocket. Otherwise I would have given her every penny I had.

In between the tears and the explanation of her problem, Lisa said to me, "Pastor, I have nothing!" That morning I had preached the message of this book. So I said to her, "Lisa you do have something to work with, let's ask God to show you what it is." Then the two of us briefly closed our eyes and prayed a short prayer. I asked the Lord to simply show her the "nothing" she had for Him to work with. I could see a spark of hope glimmer in her eye, then she left.

On this particular Sunday there was an evening service. I was hanging out in the lobby and in walks Lisa. The tears are gone and she's beaming with joy. "Pastor, Pastor," she said. "You will never guess what happened after we finished praying!" "What happened?" I said to her. She told me as she was walking out of the church, a lady in the congregation noticed the beautiful bookmarker she had in her Bible. The woman approached her and said, "What a beautiful bookmarker! Where can I purchase one?" Lisa responded, "Oh, these bookmarkers are something I just make as a hobby." The woman, overcome with excitement, started to call people over to see the bookmarker Lisa made. In a matter of seconds, there were dozens of people gawking at her bookmarkers. And, guess what? They all wanted to buy one. In that moment, Lisa received orders for bookmarkers that wiped out her supply at home and would keep her busy making more for a few weeks. She exclaimed, "Pastor, I have more than enough money for my sons' lunches this week, God has blessed me so abundantly!" Her nothing of a bookmark tucked away in her Bible was indeed something.

See the problem with our "little" is we devalue it to the point we neglect it into oblivion. We never see it—we overlook it. In our eyes it's nothing! It's so unassuming we would never think or believe God could use it to meet our need. We sometimes fail to see how God sees. In most cases, it takes God Himself to point out what we have that He wants to use. There are numerous instances in the Bible that illustrate this point and truth. For example, the call of Moses in the book of Exodus.

Exodus 4:1–5 reads,

> *Moses answered, "What if they do not believe me or listen to me and say, 'The LORD did not appear to you'?"*
>
> *Then the LORD said to him, "What is that in your hand?"*
>
> *"A staff," he replied.*
>
> *The LORD said, "Throw it on the ground."*
>
> *Moses threw it on the ground and it became a snake, and he ran from it. Then the LORD said to him, "Reach out your hand and take it by the tail." So Moses reached out and took hold of the snake and it turned back into a staff in his hand. "This," said the LORD, "is so that they may believe that the LORD, the God of their fathers— the God of Abraham, the God of Isaac and the God of Jacob—has appeared to you." (NIV)*

In this passage God has called Moses to be a deliverer for His people. His mission is to go to Pharaoh, the most powerful political leader in the world, and tell him to free the Israelites. Not only that, he is to go to the elders of Israel and tell them what God has sent them to do. Moses is no dummy; he knows there's a good chance when he tells them what God has said they might think he has inhaled too much sagebrush smoke on the backside of the desert. So to help him out, God asks him a question. "What is it you have in your hand?" Moses replies, "A staff." Moses might as well have said "nothing"! Because in a million years he had no idea the rod he had held in his hand every day for years would become the "Rod of God." A vehicle of nothing that God would use to work great miracles and bless His people in ways unimaginable. The point I'm making here is this: It took God to point out to Moses the extraordinary gift of nothing Moses had in his possession. Let me give you one more example.

A widowed mother of two comes to Elisha the prophet pleading with him for help. Her situation is dire, she is about to lose her home and her sons to her creditors. 2 Kings 4:1–2 reads,

> The wife of a man from the company of the prophets cried out to Elisha, "Your servant my husband is dead, and you know that he revered the LORD. But now his creditor is coming to take my two boys as his slaves."
>
> Elisha replied to her, "How can I help you? Tell me, what do you have in your house?"
>
> "Your servant **has nothing** there at all," she said, "except a small jar of olive oil." (NIV, emphasis added)

In order to help her Elisha asks her, "*What do you have in your house?*" Her reply, "*Your servant has nothing there at all, except a small jar of olive oil.*" Did you catch that? She lamented, "I have *nothing*, except a little oil!" We are going to talk more about this story in a following chapter. However, for now there are three things that are crucial to understand. One, she had underestimated the gift God had placed in her possession. Two, Elisha helped her to understand what she and God had to work with. Three, the nothing (her little oil) became something, and her something became everything!

So the life-changing question for you is, what do you have in your hand? Or what's in your house? Or in the words of Jesus, how many loaves do you have?

The disciples, Moses, and the widow woman all believed they had nothing in their possession that was adequate to meet the need they were facing. They were all convinced their little or nothing substance would be swallowed in one gulp by the "giant need" monster they were facing. They were thoroughly persuaded of this reality deeply in their hearts and their minds. They were certain that they were in a losing battle. However, was their perception true? Absolutely not!

The reality was, they all had what they needed to adequately meet the crisis they were facing. God had already given them something, even though they were unaware what it was. And God was eagerly waiting to partner with them to create a miracle of nothing to everything! If you and I are going to identify the gift God has given us, we must change the way we believe.

In our hearts and mind, the thinking that we have nothing in our possession for God to use mightily has to go! With God's help we then can adapt a reality based upon what the

Bible teaches and not what our own circumstances or experiences dictate. A reality that believes, *God has already provided me with what I need for a miracle to begin, and He is faithful to be with me and guide me throughout the entire process.* Let's pause here for a moment of prayer. Please pray with me,

> *Lord, I am sorry for believing and thinking in a way that limits your working through my life. Please forgive me. Help me to believe and know in my heart and mind that you have provided me with an extraordinary gift/s that you will use for your glory. Now, Lord, please open my eyes and help me discover the gift that you have already placed in my hands. In Jesus's name—Amen!*

Now that you've asked God to help you discover the something He has given you. It is time for you to discover it! Here are a few good places for you to begin your search. This by no means is an exhaustive list, however, it's designed to prompt you to look in some places you may be overlooking.

Read through this list prayerfully, reflectively, trusting the Holy Spirit to shine a spotlight on the very gift in your life God is desiring to use. God is faithful, and just like He made it clear to the disciples, Moses, and the widow woman, what He wanted to use. He will do the same for you. Time to start the search:

1. ***Your spiritual gifts and talents.*** *Therefore you do not lack any spiritual gift as you eagerly wait for our Lord Jesus Christ to be revealed* (1 Cor. 1:7, NIV). A spiritual gift is a special ability God has given you to serve Him and others with. God has blessed you with spiritual gifts and talents.

Could it be that your gift of nothing could be a talent or gift you have simply overlooked? Look again.

2. **Your finances.** *Now he who supplies seed to the sower and bread for food will also supply and increase your store of seed and will enlarge the harvest of your righteousness. You will be enriched in every way so that you can be generous on every occasion, and through us your generosity will result in thanksgiving to God* (2 Cor. 9:10–11, NIV). Your finances are a gift from God, and all that He gives you is not meant purely for your consumption. You may be amazed at how your giving can open up the heart of God in others so that miracles can begin to pour forth.

3. **Your prayers.** *Therefore confess your sins to each other and pray for each other so that you may be healed. The prayer of a righteous person is powerful and effective* (James 5:16, NIV). Your prayers are powerful. A whole nation was changed because one man prayed. Don't minimize the power of your prayers. Who knows what God will do and how powerfully He will answer you!

4. **Your ideas.** There was a lady in our church who shared with us the idea of helping a group of neglected women in Nigeria by buying a cassava grinding machine. Purchasing the machine would help them generate income by providing them work and a needed product to sell. Our church bought the machine, and her plan worked. If the idea hadn't been presented, the need may not have ever been met. Now these sweet women are experiencing great blessing because someone had a little idea. Do you have an idea swirling around in your heart and mind?

5. *Your testimony*. If God has done something in your life, your testimony can be a literal lifeline for someone else. The words you share with someone may be what they need more than anything else. The story of Naaman, the powerful Syrian commander who had contracted leprosy, conveys this truth. He had everything money could buy. However, he was losing his health and he lacked a relationship with God. He was a goner except for the testimony of the servant girl taken captive from Israel. She simply said if he were in Samaria the prophet would heal him (2 Kings 5:3). Her testimony saved his life and brought him close to the true and living God. For Naaman, her little testimony proved to be everything!

6. *Your experience and wisdom.* If you're breathing, you have experience and wisdom to share with someone. A factory owner had a machine that malfunctioned, and the staff mechanics were unable to fix it. The longer the machine failed to function the more money he lost by the minute. The owner was forced to call in a mechanistic guru who he believed could help fix the problem. The guy came and within fifteen minutes the problem was solved. He charged the owner over $10,000 for the call. The owner balked at the bill. The guru responded to his angst saying, "You're not paying me for how long I have been here; you're paying for what I know and for getting your plant back in operation." You have wisdom and experience that will help someone get their life back in action. You've been there, you know where the problem lies, and it won't take weeks to disseminate the wisdom they need

for their lives. What you know and have experienced can be used by God to bring great blessing into someone's life.

7. ***Your relationships.*** Truthfully God never calls us to do a work for Him alone. Even if we are on the other side of the world, God always has somebody somewhere praying for us. Incredible miracles happen when people work together. Ask yourself, who has God placed in my life who has a similar burden? Perhaps that relationship is what God wants to work through to make your nothing become everything.

8. ***Your love.*** The world needs love, and you have it to give. Why? Because you are a child of the great lover of all people—God! What tangible act of generosity is the Lord asking you to share in order to display His love to those around you? Remember, it may seem small, but so were the loaves and fish!

I've got a sneaking suspicion that, as you have read through our list, something you never suspected has surfaced to the front of your heart and your mind. You might even be saying to yourself at this moment, "Really God?" To which He is probably responding, "Yep!" See my friend, this is not meant to be some hard puzzle where you have to find hidden missing pieces to assemble. It is a clear-cut process, and is easy to figure out. There is a 99.9 percent chance that what is on your heart right now is the very thing God wants you to grasp in your hand for a miracle to happen—it is your nothing! Yes, it may be very small, but it is highly concentrated.

One time I was doing the laundry, and as usual I poured a

cup of detergent into the washer, turned on the machine, and went upstairs. An hour or so later I went downstairs only to find the machine and the floor covered in suds. The first thing that came to my mind was, money! Either I needed to buy a new washer or call the repairman. So I yelled upstairs to my wife, "Honey, the washing machine is on the fritz—it's loaded with suds!" She asked me, "How much soap did you put in the machine?" I told her, "a cupful as usual!" She then said, "That's concentrated detergent; all you need is a quarter of a cup."

See the something you now have in your hands is heavily concentrated. The potential is unlimited. However, one thing is necessary. As long as your nothing stays in your hand, nothing will happen. Just like loaves and fish. If those small portions of food had remained in the little boy's or the disciples' hands, that would have been the end of the story. The same goes for you and me as well. Identifying our resource is very important and it is what God wanted you to do! But for the miracle to happen you have to take what's in your hand now and place it in the hands of the One who makes all things possible. Are you ready for that handoff?

JOURNAL A LIST

Find a quiet place and take out your journal or pad of paper and list all of the gifts and talents God has blessed you with. When you finish, voice to God how you feel about what He has given you.

Chapter 7

Movement Six:

FROM YOUR HANDS TO HIS HANDS

"Bring them here to me," he said.
MATTHEW 14:18 (NIV)

O ur natural human tendency is to hold tightly to what we possess. We've all felt this a time or two, our fingers slowly tighten around our prized valuables. We've experienced our hearts shudder at the thought of opening our hand and giving to God what's in our possession. We reason that when we give, we've lost. And what we've lost will never be recovered or replaced. So we find ourselves working hard to keep what we have, as opposed to letting go and experiencing the joys and blessings that are found by placing it in the palm of another.

The truth of the matter, my friend, is miracles will never happen in yours and my hand alone. Miracles only happen when the hand of Jesus is present to work. If you and I hold on to what God has gifted us with, the miraculous process will be short-circuited, restricted by our limited human ability. However, placing our small gift in Jesus's hand allows Him to direct and orchestrate incredibly divine possibilities. Wonderful works far beyond what our hands could accomplish alone. Therefore, if we want to see nothing become everything, an important movement is necessary and needed. That is, for you and I to take the little that we have in our hand, and place it in the hands of Jesus. Remember, once Jesus helped the disciples identify the gift in their possession, He commanded them to bring the gift to Him. The same goes for you and me. Now that you know what you have in your hand, Jesus says to you, *"Bring it here it to me. I can do way more with that than you can!"*

Capable Hands

With 5.2 seconds left in the ballgame, the Chicago Bulls trailed Utah Jazz 86–85 in the 1998 NBA Finals. Like hundreds of times in the past the Bulls resorted to their number one strategy: Get the ball to Mike. Prior to this game, Michael Jordan had made twenty-four last-second game-winning shots. And he was about to do it again.

Jordan steals the ball and takes it up court. He then makes a crossover move, gives a little push, and sends Brian Russell sliding across the floor in the opposite direction. He then pulls up, and as if time slows to a crawl, he goes up in one fluid move into his trademark jump shot. The moment it leaves his hand you know where it's going. And you're right—*pump*—down it goes. Chicago Bulls win 87–86! Once again Michael Jordan proved to have the most capable hands on the court.

Like the Bulls, you and I have a go-to person, and He is not just the best on the court—He has the most capable hands in the *universe*. He is the ultimate victor, eternally faithful to all who dare trust Him with what they have.

Jesus lovingly and powerfully contends for the well-being of human souls, for the provision of our deepest needs. He fights so that the chains of darkness will be broken off captive souls, so we can live our lives free from the power of sin and death. He works miracles so that you, I, and others can have life and have life more abundantly (John 10:10). His very weakness is His strength, His nothing became everything to the universe.

There's a small verse tucked away in the Gospel of John that gives us a brief glimpse at the capable hands of Jesus and the magnitude of how many lives He touched in a miraculous way. Commenting on Jesus's three and a half years of earthly ministry, John makes this insightful statement, *"Jesus did many other things as well. If every one of them were written down, I suppose that even the whole world would not have room for the books that would be written"* (John 21:25, NIV). That statement, my friend, is mind boggling! Think of it. In just a short period of time, the hands of Jesus performed so many miracles they couldn't all be counted! This ought to encourage you and me, knowing that Jesus is reaching His hand open to us to receive our small token so that He can exceed our wildest expectations. As Ephesians 3:20 boldly states, *"Now to him who is able to do immeasurably more than all we ask or imagine, according to his power that is at work within us"* (NIV).

And think of this—His story isn't done. We are living it today.

To boost your confidence a bit more in God's ability to perform a miracle with your nothing. Let me remind you of a few "little unassuming things" God used in Scripture to do great things with.

1. He used a shepherd's staff to part a Red Sea.

2. He used a little oil in a jar to sustain a widow's household.

3. He used a little oil and flour to provide food for three people until a famine ended.

4. He used a muddy river to cleanse a leprous dignitary.

5. He used four lepers to save a city from an over-powering army.

6. He used a stone and a sling to slay a giant.

7. He used a jawbone of a donkey to slay 2,000 Philistines.

8. He used water to make wine.

9. He used five loaves of bread and two fish to feed a multitude of thousands.

10. He used one wooden cross to redeem the world.

And the list goes on…

Right now you may feel like shouting—hallelujah! However, as nice as it is to give a shout, God's after more than that. He's after the very thing you are holding in your hand. He wants you to hand it over! You and I know He's capable, so what might be stopping us from making the handoff?

Handoff Stoppers

Knowing what to do is one thing. Doing what we know to do is an entirely different story. That being the case, we must ask ourselves the question, why is it that we haven't, or are having a hard time placing finances, the gift, or ideas back into the hands of the One who gave it to us in the first place? Here are a few common reasons. See if any of these reasons resonate with you.

One: Ownership Confusion

Many times we can be guilty of making the mistake of thinking that what we have belongs to us. We say things like, *"this is my business, my ministry, my car, my house, etc."* And on a cursory level those things are yours and mine. However, they are not ours to possess and hold tightly. They are actually a gift to us from God. So, ultimately, what we have great or small is from His hand, and we are His stewards over what He has entrusted to us. Not the principal owners, just temporary stewards who have the responsibility of being faithful with what He has entrusted to us for this season of our lives. So when we are persuaded to believe that what we possess is solely ours, it makes it difficult to give back to God that which is really His in the first place. When you understand what you have is His, it makes placing it in His hand a whole lot easier. I have heard countless stories of business owners, pastors, and parents who came to the place of understanding that all their possessions belonged to God. They then placed them in His hand, and what they were unable to do in their own power, God, blew their minds by what He did through His power. Is there something you are holding on to that you think belongs to you?

Two: Fear

In Matthew 25:13–28 (NKJV), we have the Parable of the Talents. In that story the master gives each one of his servants a certain amount of talents. To one servant he gives five talents. To another he gives two, and to the last servant he gives one. The master then goes on a journey with the expectation that each servant will act faithfully and diligently with the gift that has been entrusted to them.

When he returns, the servant who was given five talents and the servant who was given two talents performed brilliantly, and they were rewarded. The servant who was given only one talent, failed miserably, and he was to be punished. The reason for his failure was voiced by his own admission. One, he made it clear he really didn't know his master. And two he was *afraid,* so he hid his talent (Matt. 25:24–25).

Fear is a powerful driving force. In this instance it prevented the servant from placing his talent in the right place. Likewise, if we allow fear to drive our lives, we will never place what God has given back in His hand so He can use it. Think of how many people are walking around the planet with God-given ideas but are afraid to execute them. Imagine how many people can sing like angels, communicate the gospel effectively, and have the means to give incredibly, but never do because fear forbids them to do so. This is nothing new, and it doesn't mean that you and I are subhuman because fear presents an obstacle for us. If anything, it should encourage us, because we are in the same company of all the greats God used in the Bible. All of them experienced fear. However, like many of them, we can allow God to help us overcome it! So a good piece of advice is to not only put your gift in God's hand, but put your fear there too. He'll take both of them.

Three: Inadequacy

Oftentimes when we reflect on the majesty and the magnificence of God, all we have and are seems dwarfed by His holy presence. We feel unworthy and undeserving. Our hearts trouble us because we love Him so deeply, and we are keenly aware that anything we could offer Him is inadequate. Sometimes we even find ourselves too broken and ashamed to try to offer Him anything.

Beloved, whether you know it or not, that place of emptiness is a beautiful place to be—broken before the living God. However, a lie of the enemy is that your brokenness is a reason for us not to pursue God. He attempts to make us doubt that God is longing to move through us in mighty ways. His intent is to bury us in the place of inadequacy and forever keep us from offering God what we have, keeping us from becoming a blessing maker.

One of my favorite Christmas songs is "The Little Drummer Boy." Honestly, every year when I hear that song during the Advent season, I weep. It touches my heart. "I have no gift to bring before the King, so I'll play my drum for him" touches a place that resonates in my soul. Those words capture the sentiment of my heart. *"Lord, what do I really have to offer you? I know I have nothing, but here is what I do have. Jesus, here is the sound of my drum..."*

I believe anyone who has experienced God's amazing grace in their life relates to that feeling of inadequacy. However, knowing that we are inadequate, we have to remember that we are loved, and the King wants you to play your drums for Him. Will you play?

Four: Not Knowing How

Maybe your reason is none of the above. Your only obstacle to making the movement of placing your gift in Jesus's hand is knowing how to do it? You may be on board, but all the abstract language I've been using hasn't taken you to a place where you know what concrete thing you can do yet. No need to be hard on yourself here either. After all, it's not like Jesus is physically standing before you with His hand extended so you can walk over and say, "here you are, Jesus!" However, even though that is not the case, there are concrete ways you can take what's in your hand and transfer it to His grasp.

How to Make the Handoff

Making that handoff to Jesus is simple. When Jesus told the disciples to bring the loaves and fish to Him, it was not difficult. He gave them an order that they were capable of doing. You and I are capable of bringing the gift God has placed in our hands to Jesus, just as the disciples did. Here's how:

1. *Cultivate a willing and worshipful heart.* We do not want to offer to God anything by constraint, out of duty, or by

compulsion. Our desire is to place in God's hands what we have, flowing from a heart that is in love with Him with a passion to please Him. Can you imagine the open hands of Jesus extended to receive the loaves and the fish from the disciples? The release of those pieces of nothingness were an offering to the Master. What makes an offering worship is not so much what you give, but more so the heart in which you give it. Our willingness to give to Jesus is an expression of worship. Worship from a willing heart. As my good friend Jonathan Owens says to his congregation on Sundays, "We give because we love!" Let me ask you a question, when is the last time, you took time to express to God how much you love Him? Do yourself a favor and enjoy the wonderful privilege of being with Him. Spend some time in His presence, not just asking Him for stuff or things. But spend some intimate moments loving on the one who loves you the most. Out of that place, your heart will open and a willingness to give to the Lord will deepen in your heart and your soul.

"'Hear, O Israel: the Lord our God, the Lord is one. Love the Lord your God with all your heart and with all your soul and with all your mind and with all your strength.' The second is this: 'Love your neighbor as yourself.' There is no commandment greater than these." (Mark 12:29–31, NIV)

2. *Verbally commit to God the gift you are placing in His hands.* Jesus, before he died on the cross, cried out,

"Father, into your hands I commit my spirit" (Luke 23:46, NIV). Though His Father was not visibly present, Jesus verbally committed His spirit into His Father's hands. While there's no way I want to be foolish and equate anything you or I have to offer to anything in comparison to the sacrificial offer of the Son of God, there is still a truth present. If we verbally offer something to God, He will receive it! Think of all the prayers prayed throughout history that God has answered! The reason He answered is because He heard them and received them. Can you hear the disciples saying to Jesus, "All right, Lord, here you go. This is all we have, five loaves of bread and two fish"?

Here is a simple prayer you can pray to guide you in the committal of your gift into the hands of Jesus:

Dear Jesus, I thank you for the gift _____ you have given me. I acknowledge, though it is in my possession, it belongs solely to you. Today, I joyfully and lovingly, place back into your hands the gift you have given me. I ask you to receive my inadequate offering and use it to work miracles for your glory—Amen!

Now there is one step left to go and the handoff is complete.

3. *Trust God will keep what you have placed in His hand and use it for His purposes.* Be confident. You have placed your

offering in God's hand, know that He has received it, He will keep it, and He will work His purposes through it! You already know He is capable, so take the pressure off yourself to make something happen. You have been obedient and given to Him what He has asked for, so "chill" and enjoy the rest of the journey. Whether the road is bumpy or smooth. What a relief the disciples must have felt when the burden of feeding the hungry multitude was resting in Jesus's hands and not their own! That same relief now belongs to you too! Like the apostle Paul, you know who you are believing in.

That is why I am suffering as I am. Yet this is no cause for shame, because I know whom I have believed, and am convinced that he is able to guard what I have entrusted to him until that day. (2 Tim. 1:12, NIV)

Friend, when you place what you have in Jesus's hand, be confident. And know He has it all in control and that He is going to do what only He can do to make heaven's dream happen on earth.

You have done so well so far, and you are to be commended for doing so! But, you know what? Keep reading, because your nothing is being transformed into everything. And you are going to want to know what to do before that happens. The movement discussed in the next chapter is going to help you prepare and get ready.

MAKE A DECLARATION

Jesus, right now this very moment I release into your hands what you have given to me. I acknowledge that all that I have is rightly yours. I refuse to allow fear, inadequacy, or ignorance to cause me to clutch my fist. My hand is open to give, just like your hand is open to receive. Thank you for receiving what I am handing over to you today. I declare that it will be used to further God's dream in and through my life.

Chapter 8

Movement Seven:
FROM COMPLACENCY TO STRATEGY

*Then Jesus directed them to have all the people
sit down in groups on the green grass. So they sat
down in groups of hundreds and fifties.*

Mark 6:39–40 (NIV)

A Playground

Recently, I attended a Celebration of Life service for a remarkable woman named Alberta Phillips. This woman was a pillar in our community, and she lived her life as a person whom God could get something to and through! During the service they had a segment where certain individuals shared heartfelt stories. A man I had never seen before stepped to the podium and began telling this story. He said he was sent by a larger church in the city to help this woman, Mrs. Phillips. And he confessed that at the time he was unfamiliar with the work she was doing.

He said he was there that day only because his church wanted to see how they might help.

To give the crowd a bit of background, he went on to tell about an organization Mrs. Phillips led called *Christian Women Against Crime.* The organization was dedicated to help youth in our city find the positive reinforcement they needed to complete school and to learn basic life skills. Many of the young women she served were young teenage mothers, and they would bring their children to the center with them. Mrs. Phillips knew the kids couldn't stay cooped up in a building for hours at time, so she dreamed of having a beautiful playground with great outdoor equipment for the kids to play on. Also, she envisioned a small court for the boys to shoot hoops.

He talked about the first meeting when he and the others sat around the table. Laying on the table right in front of him were two letters from her primary donors saying they would not help fund the playground. However, after a round of initial introductions, he said she began to pour out her dream of having a playground for the kids. She graphically described how much fun the kids would have and the joy and bonding that would take place with the mothers and their young kids. He went on to say he heard very few of those words because the letters staring him in the face indicated to him she had nothing to make that dream happen.

So he spoke up and said, "Mrs. Phillips, I'm sorry, but these letters say you are not going to be able to build the playground because your donors will not fund it." The gentleman then said she responded by saying, "I'm sorry, let me put those letters away." So she tucked them in a folder and said to the group, "Now, let's talk about this playground God is going to give us for these kids." That afternoon they laid out their plan and strategy for the playground, even though they had apparently nothing to work with.

The man concluded his tribute by saying that, though he went to help her, in all actuality she helped him. She taught him God that can do amazing miracles when all seems logically impossible. Within several months after that meeting, a large shoe company provided every penny to build the playground and the court so that the end product exceeded their greatest expectations.

God's dreams and miracles are supernatural, but they require a doable strategy to contain them. Jesus knew the miracle that was about to unfold. He understood that in a matter of moments, enough food to feed 15,000–20,000 people would be present. So He refused to allow the disciples to just stand around and socialize with the crowd. Neither was He going to let the multitudes stand around and talk about their hunger pains. Before the miracle happened, He had a strategy for what He would do once the miracle took place.

So to insure everyone received food, He instructed the disciples to have the multitudes of people to sit on the grass in groups of hundreds and fifties. By implementing this strategy, Jesus was making sure everyone would eat well. And the miracle would not turn into a chaotic disaster and the dream into a nightmare. Therefore, He instructed the people to sit in manageable groups, so they could be served effectively by the disciples, and nothing would be wasted.

Likewise, you will need to develop your own strategy for what God is doing and will do in your life. Even though it seems like nothing is happening right now, develop your strategy. Resist the temptation to wait until the miracle is in motion before you prepare your plan for distribution. Refuse the "God show me first, then I will act" mentality. Friend, God is working. He is moving, and so must you. And one way you can move is to overcome complacency and craft your strategy. In a moment, we'll explain how you can simply develop your own strategy. But first, I want to mention a virtue that is key to all strategies that are designed to serve God's dream. The all-important virtue is called faith, which is directly tied to a hope and an expectation that God is going to do something wonderful. See, Jesus's strategy preceded the multiplying of the loaves and the fish. He didn't wait for the motherlode to arrive first. Instead, He faithfully prepared for what was to come, so when the "everything" arrived He could distribute it effectively to the hungry multitude. This was what Alberta Phillips knew to be true.

Mrs. Phillips was confident God was going to multiply her loaves and fishes, so she acted by devising a strategy before the donor check ever came from the shoe company. Once again, this does not require rocket science, you can formulate your strategy quickly and simply. It can be as easy as putting people in groups on the grass or filling up six water pots with water so Jesus can turn them into wine. The issue is not complexity but compliance. Meaning you simply need to devise a plan for effective distribution, so **God can do the rest!**

Steps for a Strategy

I hope you won't get upset me with for oversimplifying this process, but technical doesn't necessarily mean difficult. So here are four easy steps to devise our strategy for moving forward with God's provision.

1. Pray. Ask God for wisdom to devise your plan. Proverbs 2:6 says, *"For the Lord gives wisdom; from his mouth come knowledge and understanding"* (NIV). God is willing to give you the insight to know what it is you should do in order to serve those He is desirous to bless. Let me give you one more example of how God can give you wisdom in prayer about what to do.

We had hit a $100,000 wall during the remodel of our building. Our resources were exhausted, and I was at a loss as to what to do. During prayer, the Lord put three people on my heart. He said to call them and tell them your vision and your need. One of the people I called was Pastor Rick Snow. I felt like a heel calling him, a beggar if you will. However, I knew God had given me wisdom for a strategy. So I called him. I explained our vision and told him our need. We talked about three minutes, he said he'd pray about it, and then he hung up the phone. The conversation was not eventful at all.

I thought to myself, so much for that. A few months later I was speaking in Florida, and the pastor of the church we were speaking at informed me that Pastor Snow was coming to have lunch with us. That didn't make sense to me. I wondered why in the world would he fly to Miami for lunch? I never will forget what happened the following day at lunch.

We all sat around the table at the Macaroni Grill, and Pastor Rick began explaining why he was there. He said, several months ago I was on a mountain praying about a sermon series I was preaching called, "The Generosity Factor." When my phone rang and it was Mark. He proceeded to tell me his vision and his need. When we hung up, the Lord told me, "Rick, put your money where your mouth is!" At the time we had $20,000 in our building fund, and the Lord said to give it all to Life Change. Not only that, we challenged the church and collected offerings for two months. So today on behalf of our church, I want to give Life Change a check for $100,000. I had to compose myself, I was about to run laps around the restaurant. What a miracle and an incredible act of generosity from a local church. God was at work, and I didn't even know it. I was so glad I prayed and listened to the strategy God gave me!

2. *Converse with others.* Chances are, others have done what you are attempting to do, or they just may be people who have a gift of wisdom who can help you. Talk with them, pick their brains for ideas. Share your vision and ask them what they would do. Over the years I have faced a lot of challenges. Many answers to those problems have been solved through conversations with others. God speaks to us and gives us His wisdom through the healthy relationships He has placed in our lives. Our relationships are a gold mine of valuable nuggets of wisdom and insight. Proverbs 15:22 says, *"Plans fail for lack of counsel, but with many advisers they succeed"* (NIV). Like the saying in the hood goes, *"If you don't know, you better ask somebody!"*

3. *Write it out.* On a piece of paper, or on your tablet or

computer, write out your plan. A group of pastors in Portland got together and wrote a plan to help their community that didn't even take up a full sheet of paper. Talk about a simple plan! That plan was so successful, the impact of the miracle God poured out impacted the neighborhood, the judicial system, the police department, the lives of many kids, and the list goes on.... A simple outline to follow to aid you in your writing centers around answering two questions. The first question is, *"What is it that I believe God wants me to do?"* The second question is, *"What is it that I need to do in order to distribute to others what I have to offer?"* You may come up with one or two activities that will be necessary or you may come up with seven. List only what you think will be absolutely necessary. You can always adjust your plan later, and chances are you will need to. But for now keep it streamlined and simple.

4. *Do it!* Now that you have a strategy, start to put it into action. Sure, there may be some things you are prohibited from doing at the moment due to a lack of resources. Don't worry about that! Do all you can right now with what you have, and the rest will follow. Remember, nothing transforming to everything begins not with what you don't have, but with what you do have. Now you have a strategy—work it!

Don't think it strange if your strategy feels a bit uncomfortable or clumsy at first—that's ok. Just keep working at it, and tweak it here or there when you need to. No strategy is ever in stone. After a while you will have it locked in, and you will be ready when your five loaves and two fish are transformed into a massive feast.

But until the provision arrives, keep your focus in the

right place. Know there will be many distracting forces that will seek to divert your attention to focus on the wrong thing. This is the reason this next movement is so critical. What you will learn in the next movement will help you keep your eyes exactly where God wants them to be—focused on an awesome place where miracles are not restricted, but released.

Focused on God Himself.

A PRAYER FOR WISDOM

God, it is your dream, and it is your resource. Help me to be a blessing maker. I ask that you will give me your wisdom to develop a solid strategy that will not allow any of the miracle you perform to be wasted. Thank you for hearing and answering my prayer. In the wonderful name of Jesus. Amen.

Chapter 9

Movement Eight:
FROM LOOKING DOWN TO LOOKING UP

He took the five loaves and two fish,
lifted his face *to heaven in prayer.*
MATTHEW 14:19 (MSG, emphasis added)

W hen I began pastoring our church, we started an out-
reach where we gave out turkeys to needy families in our
community for Thanksgiving. Each year, we generally
gave out anywhere from fifty to one hundred fowl. This particular year had been very rough financially. There was no way our
church was going to be able to afford dozens of turkeys. Even
though the place we bought them from usually gave us a great
discount, the price was still out of our reach.

That Friday, six days before we usually distributed the
turkeys, my wife and I were driving up to Seattle to attend a
conference on generosity. On our way up to the conference, we
both were disappointed because we could not give turkeys

away this year. We were bummed, and kind of silently consented to defeat. Believe me, if we'd had the money in our account we would have paid for all the turkeys in a heartbeat—but we were personally in a very tight financial place. So both of us just prayed about it and left it there. We accepted the fact we couldn't help the families who were counting on us and proceeded to the conference, unaware that God was going to give me a healthy lesson about His generosity.

That night at the conference, when the speaker finished speaking, he invited people who had a need to come to the altar to pray. At first, I wasn't going to go. I reasoned, things are pretty tight right now in our household, but God will take care of us, so I stayed seated. A few minutes later, I started thinking about the turkeys. So I got out of my seat and walked to the front of the church. And I can tell you, my total focus was heavenward, I was dialed in on God. Honestly, I was almost oblivious to the many people standing around me.

Then after a few minutes of standing and praying, I felt a couple of people place something in my pockets. I didn't even stop praying to see who they were. After the service ended, my wife and I went back to the hotel. When we got back to the room, I emptied out my pockets, and the Lord had provided us with a few thousand dollars—enough to buy all the turkeys we needed and a few extras too! That night I learned a powerful lesson that has stuck with me throughout my ministry, and for my private life as well. The lesson—when in need, do like Jesus: Look to heaven and trust your Father to provide.

In this movement, Jesus is doing something very powerful.

In His possession He has the loaves and the fish, however, before He begins the miracle of multiplication, His first move is to lift His face toward heaven. As if to say, "Father, this is your moment, do what only you can do, and work powerfully to show your immense love to all who are present here today!"

Can you imagine being present with Jesus at that very moment? Watching Him lift His face toward His Father. Seeing His eyes peering past the need of the moment and the faces of the crowd. Watching Him looking steadfastly into heaven's eyes. Believing and knowing a powerful miracle is unfolding in the midst of unsurmountable need. Wouldn't it have been great to be there?

Well, my friend, you and I weren't there because God wants us to be exactly where we are right now! He has ordered the boundaries of your habitation. You are strategically placed in your station in the world for such a time as this! God's intent is for those who share your space in life to experience and taste the goodness of His mercy and grace. Listen to this,

And He has made from one blood every nation of men
to dwell on all the face of the earth, and has determined
their preappointed times and uthe boundaries of their
dwellings. (Acts 17:26, NIV)

God is so good—He made sure you and I didn't miss that moment because He included Jesus's actions in the passage. They are on the score so you and I can imitate what He did in our own life's context. Matthew 14:19, tells us Jesus's first action was to lift His face toward heaven. This is a no-brainer because miracles come from heaven. Therefore, we, like Jesus, should fix our gaze on the One who is the source from whom all blessings flow.

The Language of Your Eyes

Lifting your eyes to heaven is more than a physical posture. Looking to heaven is a posture of the heart that speaks volumes to God about how much you value His partnership in the process. When we fail to look up to God, we are saying by our actions, "God, I have this all in control, I can get by without your help." True, you or I may be able to cling to that philosophy for a while, maybe even accomplish a few feats "for" God. But it will not allow God to work for us—we would not experience God's dream flowing through our lives. Nor would we experience the gracious blessing God is waiting to pour out on our lives. Living with a focus away from God is going to shortchange us in the long run. And who knows how many others it will shortchange too?

When we follow Jesus's example and look to heaven, we are making a powerful statement to God, a statement of trust and relationship that He delights in. By lifting our eyes to Him, we are acknowledging:

1. *God, you are my source!* All the help I need comes for you. In other words, your mantra is, *"If God fails to show up. I'm sunk!"* Honestly, without exaggeration there is a verse I quote to God and my own heart at least fifty times a year. The passage reminds me that God is my source, and I find comfort from each word when I am in need of His assistance. The words of

Psalms 121 may help you like they have helped me over the years to keep my focus on the Lord. Listen to these words and allow them to penetrate you heart and affect your gaze.

> *I lift up my eyes to the mountains—where does my help come from? My help comes from the* LORD, *the Maker of heaven and earth. He will not let your foot slip— he who watches over you will not slumber; indeed, he who watches over Israel will neither slumber nor sleep. The* LORD *watches over you—the* LORD *is your shade at your right hand; the sun will not harm you by day, nor the moon by night. The* LORD *will keep you from all harm—he will watch over your life; the Lord will watch over your coming and going both now and forevermore.*
> Psalm 121:1–8 (NIV)

2. *God, you are my treasure!* There are instances when miracles can result in material blessings and resources. However, for the one who looks to God, those blessings never become the treasures of their heart. A miracle of nothing to something is not about the acquisition of stuff. You don't need God to get stuff. But you and I do need God to attain the treasures of heaven that will transform our lives and the lives of others. Matthew 6:19–24 gives us a good admonishment and some encouragement along these lines.

> *Do not store up for yourselves treasures on earth, where moths and vermin destroy, and where thieves break in and steal. But store up for yourselves treasures in heaven, where moths and vermin do not destroy, and*

where thieves do not break in and steal. For where your treasure is, there your heart will be also.

The eye is the lamp of the body. If your eyes are healthy, your whole body will be full of light. But if your eyes are healthy, your whole body will be full of darkness. If then the light within you is darkness, how great is that darkness!

No one can serve two masters. Either you will hate the one and love the other, or you will be devoted to the one and despise the other. You cannot serve both God and money. (NIV)

So, my friend, no matter how much God blesses you to bless others, always remember where your true treasure lies, and most of all, remember the One who is your genuine treasure: God Himself.

3. *God, I am depending on you!* Jesus looked to the Father because He was dependent upon Him for His every action. The miracle of the loaves and fish was not something Jesus did independently on His own initiative. His actions were dependent on the Father's will and purposes. One of the greatest temptations you can face reading a book like this is running off half-cocked believing we can do anything we desire. The truth of the matter is, we are dependent upon God. Therefore, all we can truly see happen is what He desires—not my will, but thine, O Lord! That being said, the other side of the coin is that He desires to do more through our lives than we can fathom! So by looking to Him in utter dependence, get ready for the ride of your life!

Jesus gave them this answer: "Very truly I tell you, the

Son can do nothing by himself; he can do only what he sees his Father doing, because whatever the Father does the Son also does. For the Father loves the Son and shows him all he does. (John 5:19–20, NIV)

Little Eyes

When my youngest son, Myles, was about three years old, I took him to get his immunization shots. He didn't have a clue about the pain he was about to experience. I'll never forget when the nurse gave him the first shot. When the needle pierced his tiny arm, he didn't say a word. His little eyes just lifted up to place where I was standing, and his one glimpse said it all! His gaze was saying, *Daddy, that hurt! Will you please help me?* While I had to let him finish getting his shots, my heart was almost moved to tears. So I held him a bit tighter and spoke as many loving and encouraging words as I could muster. I was trying with all I had to comfort and help my little fellow.

Whenever I remember that time in the doctor's office with my son, I reflect upon God's love for me as His child. It makes me wonder how Father God's heart responds when He sees the eyes of His children peering to Him out of a place of pain or need. I wonder, if my son's gaze into my eyes affected my heart that much, what happens when we make eye contact with our Heavenly Father? He loves us more than an earthly person could love us, and His heart of love and compassion toward each one of us is far deeper and far wider than we could ever understand. While I may not be able to articulate all the nuances of my ruminations, one thing is certain: When our eyes connect with our Heavenly Father's eyes, we can know for certain He is going to help us!

So are you looking up? No one can make this move for you. However, I have to let you know—if you haven't looked up yet, please do so. Why? Because there are a loving pair of eyes from heaven peering down on you. Eyes that are looking for an opportunity to help you, bless you, and make everything possible out of nothing (2 Chron. 16:9). He's just waiting for you to look up to heaven and make eye contact with a physical gaze and a prayerful heart.

Jesus looked to heaven, so why don't you and I follow His example and do the same?

Those who make it this far are entering a special place where God's provision and dream begin to meet the needs of our world and community. But our journey toward becoming a blessing maker is not over yet—and the next movement will hit some of us hard.

A PHYSICAL ACTIVITY

Place a reminder on your phone to signal you to look up to heaven during the day. Physically direct your face toward the clouds, but more so, allow your soul to express to God your need and dependency upon Him.

Chapter 10

Movement Nine:
FROM CURSING
TO BLESSING

He blessed and broke and gave the loaves
to the disciples; and the disciples
gave to the multitudes.
MATTHEW 14:19 (NKJV)

This movement is a game-changer! An accelerant that will help fuel your nothing into a provisional fire of God's sufficiency and blessing. Holding in His hand the insufficient loaves and fish, Jesus did the unimaginable—He blessed them! He consciously made the decision to bless and not curse or grumble over the insufficient meal He had before Him to feed the thousands of hungry people. By blessing the loaves and fish, Jesus declared the bread and fish adequate—enough provision from the Father to meet the need!

You and I have a critical choice to make as well. One, will we curse the seemingly insufficient means gifted to us by our grumbling, murmuring, or complaining. And, in essence, tell God how worthless are the loaves and the fish He has given us to work with. Or, will we, like Jesus, be bold and dare to bless what we have. And by doing so, experience God's blessings beyond our wildest imagination and dreams. The choice is yours and mine to make!

You and I have been given by God the permission to bestow blessing upon what He has placed in our possession. Think about it for a second. You and I pray and give thanks for our daily food, asking God to bless it. If a church builds a building, the community dedicates it for God's purposes and glory. You complete a project, and before you submit it, you ask God to bless your efforts. So why not do the same for your loaves and fish? This is not some hyper-spiritual trick or gimmick! But blessing what you have is a genuine gift and privilege God gives to the person whose heart is in sync with His purpose and His will. You're not blessing what you have in attempt to manipulate God into giving you what you want. You're blessing what you have for the purpose of accomplishing what it is that He desires.

In musical terms allow me to explain this way: Cursing your nothing is like singing a dirge. A dirge is a mournful song of lament, expressing grief and deep sadness. Generally, the only time you will hear a dirge is at a funeral. The nature of the song will cause you to bury your chin into the depths of your bosom and mourn. Kind of like the way you feel when great need has worked you over, and your hope for a good tomorrow or a better outcome has left the premises.

When you make the decision to bless what you have in

your possession, it's as if your song changes. The minor and diminished notes disappear. And a joyful, hopeful faith-filled melody begins to fill your heart! The new melody drowns out the dirge, proclaiming, "God will work through my insufficiencies."

Are you ready to sing a new melody over the loaves and fishes before you? Then let me share with you a few ways you can bless what God has given to you, starting with prayer.

Bless What You Have By Praying

Our kids' education has been a hodgepodge of public schools, home schooling, and Christian schools. When our two girls were in grade school, there was a great Christian elementary school down the street from our house that my wife and I felt the Lord wanted our daughters to attend. We knew it would be a real financial stretch to make it work, and the numbers, on paper at least, were not jiving. However, through my wife and I praying together and talking with a few of our close friends, we felt it was God's will for our kids to go to the school. So, we enrolled them for school and decide to trust the Lord to work it out.

The first couple of months were great, and somehow we manage to squeak out the extra $450 a month and still eat and pay the rest of our bills. But the following months were no joke! Financially it wasn't working, and my wife and I were one centimeter away from pulling them out of the school. We were both heartbroken to make the decision, but we just couldn't afford the tuition. At that time all my wife and I had was *the desire* to keep our girls in the school, but we lacked the means to do so.

One night we were both praying at the church about our dilemma. Marla was in tears, and I was shaking my head, saying inside, *"O Lord, help us. There is no way this school situation is going to work."* I had my arm around my wife when a lady who was visiting from a country in Africa came and placed her hand on the shoulders of my wife and I. She began to pray a beautiful prayer asking God to bless us and give us the desires of our hearts. During her prayer, it felt like a logjam in my heart broke—and in my wife's heart too. We both felt God had heard our prayer and was somehow going to provide for our girls to stay in the Christian school.

A few weeks passed. The school bill was due, and we had no money. However, we had prayed, and the desire we had in our hands and in our heart had been blessed by our prayers and the prayers of the African woman. We had no idea where the money was going to come from, and in the back of our minds, pulling the girls out of the school was looking like reality. However, at the time the bill was due a man from our church said God had placed it on his heart to help our kids with school. We had not said anything about our need to anyone in our church. He gave us a check for $500, fifty dollars more than we needed and just enough to pay our tithes on the amount. From that time forward, every month we had the finances to pay the tuition for our girls, and they both had a great experience at the school. In hindsight, it was God's dream for them.

One of my favorite verses on prayer is Philippians 4:6–7, which reads,

Do not be anxious about anything, but in every situation, by

prayer and petition, with thanksgiving, present your requests to God. And the peace of God, which transcends all understanding, will guard your hearts and your minds in Christ Jesus. (NIV)

A good way to paraphrase this verse is like this, *"Don't worry about anything, but pray about everything!"*

Not having enough, as you already know, can and will create a world of worry to flood our hearts and mind. Worry is as bad as cursing what you have. It is unprofitable, unfruitful, and unproductive. The only thing it is good for is to make you sick and tired, and who wants that! God extends an invitation to us to pray to Him about our nothing. And when we do, His peace will fill and protect your heart and mind from all the assaults that seek to short-circuit His miracle flowing through your life. So if you find yourself worrying about what you don't have, use it as a note to remind you to pray God's blessing on what you do have. And along side your prayers, verbally blessing what you have is powerful too!

Verbally Bless What God Has Given You

A friend of mine had purchased a parcel of land he believed would be a good financial investment. It turned out to be nothing but trouble.

Like the albatross around the sailor's neck in "The Rime of the Ancient Mariner," it seemed to haunt his prospects. When he purchased the property, he knew that the Lord had provided for him, and he had vision for the property: to use it both for his business and, more importantly, to extend God's kingdom ministry in his neighborhood.

Nothing went as planned. He was unable to do with the property what he originally envisioned. Over time, the land became both unusable *and* unsalable. The parcel of land that once filled his heart with joy and his mouth with praises, had turned sour—real sour. Eventually, he hated even to drive by the property because of the sinking feeling. There were days when he verbally expressed his angst, telling others as well as himself, "This is a lousy, worthless parcel of ground."

Then one day something happened. The Lord convicted his heart and said to him, *Why don't you stop cursing what I have given you and start blessing it?* This thought had never crossed his mind before. In fact, it seemed a bit odd: blessing something so unpleasant in his life. Nevertheless, he listened and started to bless the property. For a couple of years, a few times a week, he would go to the property and pronounce a blessing over it, a bit like Jesus blessing the loaves and fish in front of the impossible need.

Standing in front of his property, he would say the words God had placed on his heart through prayer. The word God gave him to bless his property with was:

God has blessed this property, and this property is valuable and desirable!

That was it! As far as the property goes, nothing happened immediately. But a miracle was happening—first of all, in my friend's heart. His attitude toward the property was changing, and the resident angst in his soul was being evicted. Eventually he reached a place of peace and confidence that God had everything in control, even though nothing at all had changed.

Sometime later, a stranger knocked on his door. Not knowing him, he opened the door and asked how he might help him. The man told my friend that he was a developer and he wanted to purchase his property. The first words out of Scott's mouth were, "Why? There are so many other pieces of land that are better than mine." The developer replied, "*Your property is valuable and desirable to us. It will be the anchor site for our development.*" He was floored! This man used the same exact words to describe his property that God had given him to bless his property: "*the property is valuable and desirable!*" My friend sold the property, and he was able to be a tremendous blessing to his church and to God's kingdom. He sometimes wonders what would have happened if he had not turned from his cursing to a place of blessing.

Like Jesus did, like my friend did, I encourage you to affirm your faith in God's person and power by deciding today to move from cursing to blessing what you have. Believe me, I know how hard it is to make this decision, especially when you have been faced with a need for a long time. I could spend the rest of the chapter telling you about my wounds and abrasions I've suffered over the years. However, the right thing to do is the right thing to do. So here is a simple way you can verbally bless what you have in your hands. You can prayerfully come up with your own blessing, but here is one to get you started. Simply open you heart, and offer to God you gift by praying these simple words.

God, I thank you for the gift you have placed in my

hands. Today, in Jesus's name I bless it and declare that what you have provided is sufficient to meet the needs I face, and it will be used by you to fulfill your will and your purposes. Amen!

Now for one final note of blessing.

Giving

In the same blessing movement, the Bible tells us Jesus gave what He blessed to the disciples, and the disciples gave the miraculous provision to the people. Giving what you have is a way to bless your God-given provision. The Bible tells us in Acts 20:35, *"In everything I did, I showed you that by this kind of hard work we must help the weak, remembering the words the Lord Jesus himself said: 'It is more blessed to give than to receive'"* (NIV). Let's not kid each other here, there has been a lot of abuse surrounding giving. However, the point I want to make here is that giving is a blessing, and God uses giving to empower you to bless more people (Prov. 11:24–25).

Jesus blessed and multiplied the loaves and the fish, not to create a stockpile but to get the food to the people who needed it. The way the people received the miracle was through the generosity of the little boy who initially *gave* the lunch, Jesus who *multiplied* the lunch, and the disciples who *served* the lunch.

Giving blesses what you have by opening the doors and allowing what you have to flow to others. Selfishness closes the door—after all, how much bread and fish can you and I eat? I could tell you a lot of stories to illustrate this point, but this humorous story with my oldest son shows it in an amazing way.

My son Micah was not always the most … *generous* … kid when it came to food or treats. Occasionally he might let a precious morsel slip through his fingers into the hands of a cousin or another kid.

One Sunday after church, he had gotten a pack of gum from someplace and had managed to quickly get down to his last piece. He was standing in the aisle with more wrapper than gum showing in his hand, and a lady said to him, "Hey, Micah, can I have a piece of gum?" Looking up to heaven, probably saying to himself, *O God, this lady just asked me for my last piece of gum!* So reluctantly and on his own initiative he gave her his last piece of gum. (In itself, that must have been a minor miracle.) When he gave her the gum I could see the tears building in his eyes. Even though he had eaten the other eight pieces in the last hour, he grieved that precious one that got away!

Next week after service, he came up to me and said, "Dad, she gave me a whole bag of candy. For almost two years, every Sunday after church, this lady gave Micah a small bag of candy. It got to the place that after service many of the other kids would flag him down to get some of what was in the bag. From giving one piece of gum, he became the candy man at church. It became humorous, because on some Sundays after church I would kick him out of my office, because he was trying to hold on to the stash and avoid the after-church-candy-giveaway!

You may not have a lot to give right now. But give what you have. God sees it and He will bless you for it! I love the stanza in "Joy to the World" where it says, *He comes to make his blessings flow far as the curse is found.*" Friend, you are blessing what you have in order to be redemptive. To work with God in order to release the blessing, Jesus died for a broken humanity. So from this moment on, no more singing a dirge. Speak, pray, and give. Bless what you have. Not only will you be glad you did, but so will many others!

This next movement is a bit different from all of the others. It requires you to do something many of us, including myself, have a hard time doing. Can you guess what that may be?

PHYSICAL TOUCH AND DECLARATION

Jesus physically touched what He blessed. If you can, physically place your hand on whatever your fragment maybe. If not, then write out what it is on a sheet of paper. Place your hand on the object or paper and declare God's blessing upon it. It's not about stringing together some magical words, but an expression of your trust and dependency on God. With your hand on the gift, declare:

Today, in Jesus's name, I bless _____ and declare that what you have provided is sufficient to meet the needs I face, and will be used by you to fulfill your will and your purposes. Amen!

Chapter 11

Movement Ten:
FROM WRESTLING
TO RESTING

I waited patiently for the LORD;
he turned to me and heard my cry.

PSALM 40:1 (NIV)

The Lord had given us the Craigo's building in a marvelous way. He had taken the nothing we had and made it everything we needed to buy the building. To say the least, we were absolutely ecstatic. However, after several months had passed, that excitement waned as the reality of what it would take to renovate the building set in. At first, this was not even a concern. We had great momentum, and everyone was telling me, *"Mark, we'll have no problem finding the money to get the building remodeled."* Well, they were wrong in their predictions and our momentum and excitement flew south for the winter for a very long time—seven years if you want to be exact!

We knew from the onset the building was a dilapidated

disaster. However, we didn't know the extent of it. By the time estimates were finished, it was over a million dollars' worth of disaster.

For the first few years we could not even conduct a service in our own building. For almost five years we were a vagabond church, meeting in almost any vacant place that could hold a few chairs. We moved around so much that our informal motto became, "If you can find us you can worship with us."

But the bottom line was simple: we owned the biggest building in the neighborhood, and we couldn't even use it. As time went on, the struggle to remodel the building became even more personally difficult for me than the battle I went through trying to buy it. We tried everything we could to raise money to at least start on the project. It all failed, from special offerings to capital campaigns. You name it, I did it, with the exception of holding up a piece of cardboard on the I-5 off ramp with *OUR CHURCH NEEDS MONEY* scrawled on it in black marker.

We tried to borrow money from banks. We were rejected so often, I just about developed an inferiority complex. The stress spilled into my day-to-day life. My frustration grew and grew, to the point that when I bumped into people I hadn't seen in a couple of months, I dreaded conversing with them. "How's the building coming?" I knew they'd ask. I hated that the only thing I could say was, "Nothing has changed, we're still trusting God."

During this period all the critics and experts came out of the woodworks. I heard so many times, "Mark, you should have..." and, "Mark you shouldn't have..." that I estimated that if I had a dollar for each comment, the project would have been funded.

Years of delay! The depth of the pain surprised me. It cut to the core of my heart, to a hidden place where discouragement oozed into my soul. On some of my worst days I wondered why we had even tried. *Why did I even want this building?*

As our church was going through this struggle, one of the miracles the Lord gave us was the grace to wait upon Him. He did not allow us to quit or get to the point that we were so overcome with discouragement we abandoned the vision He gave us for our community. He kept us and empowered us to wait on Him until our nothing became everything.

I confess, my natural tendency is to run ahead of the Lord. When I hear the word wait it makes me cringe. It makes me feel like telling the Lord, why wait? Come on, God, let's get this party started! But it never works. Waiting used to make me feel like something inside me is dying because I'm forced to get off of Mark's agenda and yield to God's. It does not feel good at all! All of the mental duress, the emotional roller-coaster ride, the physical stress, makes me feel like I've been in a five-hour wrestling match with the Hulk. I don't like it—waiting, at times, has worn me out! I don't know if you can relate to that, or am I the only one so unspiritual.

Although I haven't arrived, I have gotten a hair better when I have to wait on the Lord. I've learned over the years that when God has me wait, He doesn't expect me to be in a full-blown wrestling match. Nor does He expect you to be in one either. The Father wants you and I to REST while we wait—not wrestle.

Although the word *rest*, or *wait*, is not written in The Feeding of the Five Thousand, it is definitely implied. To see the rest and the waiting involved in the text, we must read the passage through the eyes of the disciples. When faced with the reality of having to feed thousands, the disciples initially had no idea how they would do it. They had to wait on Jesus for the answer to come, even though Jesus said to them, "*You give them something to eat.*" And they participated in the movements you have learned in this book. They could not rush Jesus's process. So while they were in motion carrying out the movements, they were also waiting on Jesus to provide the everything!

Likewise, while you and I are engaged in the other movements, we will be required to wait, or rest, until Jesus gives us everything. This doesn't mean we become totally inactive and do nothing. But it does mean, "*while we are moving, we are waiting!*" This can be very hard to do, but understand, waiting is a vital part of the process and a necessary movement. Remember that the goal of nothing becoming everything is not manipulation, but synchronization. Waiting allows us to be in sync with Jesus so that the miracle happens on His terms and not ours. And in the process we become more like Jesus.

As one fellow "waiter" to another, here are a few of the valuable lessons we learned through our long and sometimes dark seven-year period that may help you as you rest and wait on the Lord. Let's start with something we forget to do—remember!

1. Remember

While you and I are waiting, it is easy to forget who God is. As members of the human race, we are all susceptible to frequent bouts of short-term memory lapses. Especially when our faith is challenged, and we are forced to wait on the Lord. Our inability to see His hand at work causes His faithfulness of yesterday to become a distant memory. When we forget God, our waiting becomes arduous and much more difficult.

One day, I and three other leaders in our church were gathered in a small section of our ragged building. All of us were discouraged! We were at a loss for direction and were stuck. We felt abandoned and alone. A friend of ours named Pastor Bob was standing with us and he saw we needed encouragement. So he proceeded to tell us a story. A true story, he said, which was told to him by a wonderful servant of God who is now in heaven, named David Shock. Here's the story he told us to help us remember what we had forgotten.

There was a struggling single mother and her son who were about to be evicted from their home. A few days before they were to be evicted the mother told the little boy the story of the gold coin in the fish's mouth (Matt. 17:27). After hearing the story, the little boy flashed a big smile and went to sleep. The next morning, he went to the drawer, pulled out his piggy bank, and emptied all its contents. Putting his few pennies in his pocket, he went to the fish market. Unfortunately, all he had was enough to purchase the head of a fish. So the merchant wrapped the fish in a piece of newspaper, and the boy headed home to tell his mother he solved their financial crisis.

When he made it home he could see his mom had been crying. So he said to her, *"Hey, mom, don't cry. I bought a fish just like in the story you told about last night."* This poor mom thought, what in the world have I done. She explained to the boy what she read to him last night was a story, and that doesn't happen to everyone. When the boy left the room the mother threw the fish on the counter and wept. *"A fish head,"* she cried, *"O God, what have I done."* However, as she wept over the paper she looked in between the mouth and saw her name written in black and white. The paper read, if you know the whereabouts of this person please call this number. She picked up the phone and called the number. An attorney then informed her that her old neighbor passed. He had no relatives and he left his estate for her and her son. Pastor Bob concluded the story with an exclamation mark. He looked each one of us in the eyes and said, *"The gold coin is still in the fish's mouth!"*

We were so moved. Honestly, we wept. His story had powerfully reminded us to remember God and keep the faith. Even though nothing had changed financially, our confidence and hope were renewed because we remembered God.

Simply remembering God is a powerful confidence builder in the face of whatever giant you face while you are waiting. When David was about to fight Goliath, he knew he could overcome him because of God's past track record in his life. Listen to what he said to Saul when the king was telling him it was impossible for him to defeat the giant. David remembered God by telling Saul,

Your servant has been keeping his father's sheep. When a lion or a bear came and carried off a sheep from the flock, I went after it, struck it and rescued the sheep from its mouth. When it turned on me, I seized it by its hair, struck it and killed it. Your servant has killed both the lion and the bear; this uncircumcised Philistine will be like one of them, because he has defied the armies of the living God. The LORD *who rescued me from the paw of the lion and the paw of the bear will rescue me from the hand of this Philistine.* (1 Sam. 17:33–37, NIV)

My friend, stop right now and take the time to remember God. Pull out a sheet of paper and make a list of all the wonderful things He has done in your life. Allow what you write on your list to empower you while you are waiting. And let it give you a fresh hope to fuel your passion and dream for the future!

2. Realize

While we were waiting for the Lord to make our nothing everything, our church unintentionally adopted a motto: *"God is not just building a building, He is building His people."* This short statement was a powerful declaration, reminding us that we, God's people, are His number one priority, not the brick and mortar. Foremost on His agenda is that we become a people of character, who reflect the love of Jesus Christ to a broken world. Waiting gives God the opportunity to form Christ in us.

I'm not sure who started it, or even how it became so

widespread in our community. Although, now in hindsight, it was obvious who made sure this truth worked its way into the fabric of our church. It was the Holy Spirit who was dialing us in on what God was up to during this waiting period. See, our focus was the building—God's focus was us. If He wanted to, God could have given us the money to remodel the building in one day; however, He chose to take seven years to make it happen. Why?

When you are in a place of waiting, spiritual formation is occurring in your life. You are growing in your faith, and most of all you are provided with a wonderful opportunity to know God on a deeper level. So in the middle of your waiting, realize you are in a place of great blessing. You can become more like Jesus. You're in a God-ordained place where you can get to know Him better. And, after all, isn't that truly everything? No wonder James tell us,

> My brethren, count it all joy when you fall into various trials, knowing that the testing of your faith produces patience. But let patience have its perfect work, that you may be perfect and complete, lacking nothing. (James 1:2–4, NKJV)

3. Renew

This may seem like a no-brainer. Staying in God's presence through prayer and fellowship with the community of faith is a lifesaver. *Our battles and struggles drain our strength. God's presence renews our strength.* Only God has unlimited strength. We are collapsible. You and I can grow weary, tired, and then faint. We are incapable of enduring in our own strength; our gas tanks are not wide or deep enough for the journey. So we constantly need our strength to be renewed in the presence of God. Spending time in His presence in prayer, privately and corporately, will definitely recharge your battery. Also, spending time with other healthy Christ followers will encourage you to not give up. Your brothers and sisters, like Pastor Bob, will strengthen you to wait until nothing becomes everything. I can't tell you how many times a word spoken from the mouth of a brother or sister was used by God to strengthen me and encourage my heart! Isaiah 40:29–31 says,

> *He gives power to the weak, and to those who have no might He increases strength. Even the youths shall faint and be weary, And the young men shall utterly fall,*
>
> *But those who wait on the Lord Shall renew their strength; They shall mount up with wings like eagles, they shall run and not be weary, They shall walk and not faint.* (NKJV)

4. Rejoice

As a follower of Jesus Christ, we don't rejoice because everything is as we wish it to be, we rejoice because of who He is. Rejoicing in the Lord was one thing our church did, whether we were meeting in a tent, a school, or in a dilapidated building. Throughout those years our church would worship and praise the Lord for who He was, what He had done, and what He was going to do!

There was a song by Fred Hammond entitled, "Blessed." We sang this song so many times and so long we wore grooves in the vinyl so that the song would skip in the same spot over and over. When we made it to bridge of the song, it took us a long time to cross it. The words were, *"Late in the midnight hour, God's going to turn it around. He's going to work in your favor."* Those words, spoke powerfully to us. When it is dark, God will turn it around, and everything will work for our good. Hallelujah! That was some God news during our time of waiting. This song helped our church to hold on until our midnight passed. It helped us to know that God's time is not our time. It may be in the midnight hour, but surely He was going to come and turn it around. And as you're going to discover in a minute—He did!

Friend, the time for you to start rejoicing in the Lord is now, while you are waiting. Remember, Jesus is your reward and He is your everything. Your miracle will happen and your loaves and the fish will multiply. But until then, you have a greater reason to rejoice. Jesus Christ is the Lord of your life and He loves you. Like the Bible says in Habakkuk 3:17–18,

> *Though the fig tree does not bud and there are no grapes on the vines, though the olive crop fails and the fields produce no food, though there are no sheep in the pen and no cattle in the stalls, yet I will rejoice in the* Lord, *I will be joyful in God my Savior.* (NIV)

And for another word of encouragement, in one sentence, Philippians 4:4 tells us twice to rejoice,

> *Rejoice in the Lord always. Again I will say, rejoice! (NKJV)*

Friend, your time to rejoice is now! Jesus is present, and like the theologian Mary Poppins once said, "Just a spoonful of sugar helps the medicine go down." Well, rejoicing in Jesus is wonderful sugar while you wait.

OK I Will!

A friend mine, invited me to have coffee with him at the local Starbucks. I honestly did not want to go. Not because he was a bad guy or anything like that—in fact he is a great dude! However, I knew he was going to ask me about trying to get a loan to complete our building. As I mentioned earlier, I had tried that a thousand times to no avail. Anyway, I went to coffee with him. We sat there for about five minutes, he sipping java and me hot chocolate, when he broached the forbidden subject. "Mark," he said, I think you should try to get a loan to finish up your building." I was agitated, but I hid my emotions like a poker player. I explained to him about our repeated failed attempts to secure financing, but he wouldn't let it go. So after thirty minutes of verbal ping-pong, I consented. I said to him, "OK I will!" That was on a Friday. The following Monday, we received a call from the bank, asking if they could give us a loan to complete our building. I was shocked! Here was a bank calling and asking if they could loan us the money we needed without any solicitation from us. They did, and we finished the first phase of our building. It turned out beautiful, and it brought great esteem to a desolate neighborhood.

One of my greatest joys happened one Sunday after service. A man who had recently come to faith in Christ came to me. He said, Pastor Mark, right where you were preaching from is the exact place I used to come to buy alcohol! Now, I'm coming here not to get drunk but to hear God's Word!" This is what it was all about. The very reason God took our nothing and made it everything! Imagine what miracles God has in store for you! So don't give up—keep waiting on Jesus!

See, waiting may not be a wanted movement, but it is a *beautiful* movement. Waiting on God gives Him the room not only to work a miracle, but the space to make you more like Him. When it's all said and done, you yourself will say, "I wouldn't trade those days for anything. It was all well worth the wait." Because the Master Blessing Maker made His dream come true, and we rejoiced to see it come to pass! Now there is just one final thing left to discuss, and you are going to discover that God has one last surprise tucked away for you.

SPEAK THE SCRIPTURE

Find a quiet place and slowly read this passage. First, read it silently. Then read it out loud. Then write it for yourself while speaking the words with faith and confidence:

> I remain confident of this: I will see the goodness of the Lord in the land of the living. Wait for the Lord; be strong and take heart and wait for the Lord. (Psalm 27:13–14, NIV)

FROM NOTHING
TO EVERYTHING

So they all ate and were filled,
and they took up twelve baskets full
of the fragments that remained.
MATTHEW 14:20 (NKJV)

en would have been remarkable. Five hundred would have been jaw-dropping. Five thousand would have been beyond words. But fifteen to twenty thousand people all filled, abundantly fed by five small loaves of bread and two little fish—what a blessing. What a miracle! A miracle where Jesus took nothing (five loaves of bread and two fish) and made it something (the meal of the day), and that something then became everything (enough food to feed thousands with some left over).

Friend, the story of The Feeding of the Five Thousand does not end here. Nor is God ceasing to abundantly pour out His miracles. God wants to unleash the rivers of His blessings through you, His blessing maker.

Remember, when God decides to do an incredible work through your life, very rarely will you have truckloads of supplies initially. Just like the feeding of the multitude began with so little, chances are that's where you're starting. However, you are well on your way to experiencing life-changing miracles and blessings!

The powerful movements you've learned have changed you personally. You have re-visioned. You have seen through the eyes of God's heart how He wants to use you and what you have to bless the lives of those you love. Your heartbeat is different. It pounds to the beat of God's purposes. Settled within you is a deep conviction, that if God can get something through you, He will get it to you. Also, your thinking has changed. You no longer are a prisoner of a scarcity mentality. Your thinking has expanded to a whole new realm of possibilities. You're free to imagine and dream again because you believe God is not limited by whatever barriers you are facing. Finally, you've placed in Jesus's hand your gift, and you are blessing what you have and not cursing it. My friend, you have made great progress. And you now have what God requires of you to be a blessing maker. It is going to be exciting to watch God's dream unfold through your life.

Now for your final surprise. The one thing I forgot to mention—the leftovers.

The Bible tells us, the multitude ate and were satisfied. However, there's one more little item to mention—there were twelve baskets left over. In biblical times, when people would travel they would carry small baskets in order to take their lunch and other items. It would be equivalent to you and I carrying a small backpack. Though the Bible doesn't say this, I believe the baskets belonged to the twelve disciples. So here you have the twelve people Jesus used to get something to and something through now having bread in their own baskets. Although this wasn't the ultimate purpose, it illustrates a great truth. If you allow the Lord to use you to meet the needs of others, He will not forget you—He will meet your needs too!

When we were experiencing some of the nothing woes I shared with you in the previous pages, my family had a personal need. Our family had grown and we were cramped in the house we were living in. It was becoming impractical for a number of reasons. For three years we tried to find a house that was suitable to meet our needs. There were plenty of houses available, but they were far too expensive for us.

On one of our many house-hunting excursons, my wife and I got into one of those "blissful" marital disagreements. She wanted to look at a particular house, and I told her, "we need to be realistic; that is not going to happen!" After the last word of that sentence rolled off my bottom lip, the excursion ended and we both endured a silent ride home. And after that fiasco we didn't go house hunting any more.

Going back to our vacation on the boat, after the Lord addressed my scarcity thinking, I started believing God could give us a house. So when I made it back home, I started house hunting again. *Alone,* mind you. As I searched, nothing really grabbed my attention, until I saw a beautiful spacious white house. I pulled over to the side of the road and grabbed a flyer out of the box and went home to see what my Marla thought about it.

I walked through the door and said to her, "Hey, honey, I think I found a house you might like." So I handed her the flyer, she looked at it without saying a word. She calmly went into the bedroom and came back with the same flyer that I had told her months ago to get a reality check on. I guess I was the one who was not being realistic. But we had a problem, we still didn't have any more money than we had before.

I know you are supposed save up for a house. However, when you have nothing to save, what can you do? All we had in the bank was $300. But God blessed us. He gave my wife and I several miracles to get us into our new home. One woman, without solicitation, said God spoke to her and she gave us a $20,000 check. Another college student gave us $1,000. God gave us every penny we needed for the down payment. Then, our mortgage company at the last minute refused to finance the house. However, while sitting in church, a woman told my wife there was a friend of hers who could help us, and he did. We moved into the house and have been there for the last sixteen years. God is faithful. He gave us some bread for our own baskets. He's just kind like that!

Friend, our world is filled with broken and hurting people. God has a dream and He wants to make you a part of it. I'm praying with you and for you, that as you make these movements, people who have deep hunger will feast as God uses you to be a blessing maker by turning your nothing into something and your something into everything!

Now to him who is able to do immeasurably more than all we ask or imagine, according to his power that is at work within us. (Ephesians 3:20, NIV)

89870970R00085

Made in the USA
Columbia, SC
23 February 2018